AMERICAN CONTAGIONS

AMERICAN CONTAGIONS

Epidemics and the Law
from Smallpox to COVID-19

John Fabian Witt

Yale

UNIVERSITY PRESS

NEW HAVEN & LONDON

Published with assistance from the income of the
Frederick John Kingsbury Memorial Fund.

Yale University Press books may be purchased in quantity
for educational, business, or promotional use. For information, please e-mail
sales.press@yale.edu (U.S. office) or sales@yaleup.co.uk (U.K. office).

Designed by Dustin Kilgore.
Set in Yale type by Karen Stickler.
Printed in the United States of America.

Library of Congress Control Number: 2020940896
ISBN 978-0-300-25727-4 (hardcover : alk. paper)

A catalogue record for this book is available from the British Library.
This paper meets the requirements of ANSI/NISO Z39.48-1992
(Permanence of Paper).

10 9 8 7 6 5 4 3 2 1

For Gus and Teddy,
my heroic contagion-era companions

CONTENTS

Introduction   1

Chapter 1: The Sanitationist State   13

Chapter 2: Quarantinism in America   35

Chapter 3: Civil Liberties in an Epidemic?   61

Chapter 4: New Sanitationisms / New Quarantinisms   85

Chapter 5: Masked Faces toward the Past   107

Afterword: Viral Protests   139

Notes   143

Suggested Reading   161

Acknowledgments   165

Index   167

AMERICAN CONTAGIONS

INTRODUCTION

Salus populi suprema lex esto.
(The health of the people is the supreme law.)
— Cicero, *De legibus*

Not long ago, and for most of American history, infection was an everyday crisis. Infectious diseases like smallpox, bubonic plague, yellow fever, polio, cholera, typhoid fever, malaria, and influenza helped produce many of the defining features of the modern world: street cleaning, the shape of city neighborhoods, the clean water piped to our kitchens, and the pediatrician visits that mark the lives of our young children. Even how people behave in the bedroom in their most intimate moments reflects the risk of infectious disease.

Less tangibly, perhaps, but just as profoundly, laws and government have shaped and been shaped by recurrent crises of infectious disease. Epidemics have offered vast powers to state officials. They have produced new ideas about individual rights and basic civil liberties. They have raised questions about equality, since infections have not targeted Americans equally. And they have demanded that we create institutions capable of protecting important values while aggressively fighting the risks of infection and disease.

This book is a citizen's guide to the ways in which American law has shaped and responded to the experience of contagion. In the months after COVID-19 arrived in the United States in January 2020, Americans began immediately replaying patterns from the past. Even new responses were powerfully conditioned by history. And how could it have been otherwise? As Karl Marx once wrote, people make their own history, "but they do not make it just as they please."[1] We produce the future out of history's ingredients. But we are not doomed to repeat it, either as unnecessary tragedy or as ignorant farce. If the past is a guide, how our law responds to contagion now and in the future will help decide the course of our democracy. Historically, the law of epidemics has prompted Americans to make choices about basic values. People who know their history make better choices.

* * *

In the United States, the law of epidemics stems from the legal authority of the police power. But what is the police power? It is not the same as the "police," though police departments derive their power from it. The police power is more fundamental than the law enforcement departments that share its name. It is, as one early twentieth-century authority put it, the power of the state "to secure and promote the public welfare . . . by restraint and compulsion."[2] *Black's Law Dictionary* defines it as the "inherent and plenary power of a sovereign to make all laws necessary and proper to preserve the public security, order, health, morality, and justice."[3] The police power, in short, is the foundational authority of governments to look after the well-being of the people within their jurisdiction.

A distinguishing and often misunderstood feature of the constitutional system is that, as Justice Louis Brandeis observed in 1919, the federal government "lacks the police power."[4] By design, the framers of the Constitution established the U.S. government as a system of specifically defined powers. Some of those powers have come to be understood as giving federal officials and the Congress certain authority over questions of public health. The enumerated powers over interstate and foreign commerce are leading examples. Many jurists contend that broad enumerated powers like these offer the federal government a sweeping authority that would include virtually all questions of public health. For much of the twentieth century the Supreme Court seemed to agree.[5] But the framers did not specifically enumerate a federal police power, at least not as such, and the Tenth Amendment to the Constitution, ratified in 1791, seems to affirm the basic point: "The powers not delegated to the United States by the Constitution," it reads, "nor prohibited by it to the states, are reserved to the states respectively, or to the people." The basic police power to look after the health of the people is one of the powers so reserved.

In the absence of a federal police power, and without federal political will to act through the commerce or spending powers, legal measures in the United States to stop the spread of contagion have mostly been the product of state law. State and local governments have typically been the source for quarantines, vaccination mandates, condemnations of contagious property, and basic safety measures of countless varieties.

States, however, do not act unconstrained. For one thing, the general state police power is itself hedged in by enumerated federal powers. In the first half of the nineteenth century, courts worked out boundaries between state police powers, on the one hand, and federal power over interstate and international commerce, on the other. Moreover, the civil liberties of individuals limit what state governments can do. The federal Constitution, especially the Bill of Rights and the Fourteenth Amendment, guarantees rights such as freedom from unreasonable arrest as well as freedom of speech, religious liberty, and private property, all of which have been pitted against public health and the police power at times in American history.

* * *

The ways in which infectious disease and the law have interacted with one another constitute a principal subject of this book. For decades, historians of science and medicine have debated a related but more general question: how does infectious disease interact with human societies?

One view of the role of infectious disease in history contends that disease drives change.[6] According to this school of thought, contagion forces the world to respond. Its imperatives forge new patterns and prompt new legal and political institutions. European settlers and conquerors brought diseases like smallpox and measles that killed as many as 90 percent of the 70 million or more people living in the Americas in 1492.[7] Across the Americas, pandemic disease radically reordered authority and community. Medieval England, too, was remade when the bubonic plague killed half the population in the middle of the fourteenth century. Parliament established a new regime for conscripting labor, enforced by a new phalanx of royal officials. In such circumstances, epidemics make the state.

A contrary school of thought argues that politics makes epidemics. Existing legal and social institutions shape the ways epidemics arise. Viruses evolve to take advantage of the world as it is, and the world shapes the ways germs spread. In turn, our institutions — ones we inherit from the past — powerfully constrain the pathways of our responses to epidemic. In the United States, for example, the decentralized police power channels epidemic policy into state governments and private actors rather than the federal government. Public institutions, in this view, give direction to epidemics, not vice versa.[8]

The truth lies in between. New germs help make new laws and institutions, yet old ways of doing things shape the course of epidemics and the ways in which we respond to them. Epidemics proceed as a set of feedback loops between germs and society. And as a result, history not only tells us where we've been, it also shapes the present moment and helps determine where we are headed. To paraphrase William Faulkner, legal responses to past viruses never die; they're not even past.

* * *

Those who take this middle path in thinking about epidemics and society observe that nation-states in the modern world have tended to respond to infectious disease crises in one or both of two ways.

On the one hand, there are *quarantinist* states. Authoritarian states exercise forceful controls over the bodies and lives of their subjects, locking down communities, neighborhoods, and cities and imposing broad quarantine orders, often backed by the military. When cholera arrived in eastern Europe in the 1820s, for example, states like Prussia and Austria enforced broad bans on movement in and out of towns.

On the other hand, there are *sanitationist* states. A sanitationist state employs liberal policies designed to eliminate environments that breed disease. In London, for example, cholera's arrival in the mid-nineteenth century produced new water systems and new efforts to clean the streets. Sanitationist approaches emphasize improvement of social conditions, education, social trust, and voluntary participation in public efforts to overcome disease.

What kind of country is the United States? On the spectrum from authoritarian quarantinism to liberal sanitationism, the United States has often occupied two positions at once: one approach for those with political clout, and another for everyone else. America has always been a divided state with a mixed tradition. For middle-class white people and elites, public health policy typically reflected liberal sanitationist values. The law has protected property rights for the wealthy and attended to the civil liberties of the powerful. At the nation's borders, however, and for the disadvantaged and for most people of color, the United States has more often been authoritarian and quarantinist. American law has regularly displayed a combination of neglect and contempt toward the health of the powerless.

But that is not all. Epidemics make visible the ways in which even the ostensibly neutral and libertarian rules of American social life contain the compounded form of discriminations and inequities, both old and new. The most basic rules of American law—from the law of private property to the law of health insurance to the law of employment—structure the social experience of disease and infection.

INTRODUCTION

* * *

The future of America's mixed tradition is up for grabs in the COVID-19 pandemic. What is the relationship between individual liberty and the common good? What is the role of the federal government and what is the role of the states? Will long-standing traditions of government and law give way to the social imperatives of an epidemic? Will we let the inequities of our mixed tradition continue?

In the early days of the 2020 pandemic, the United States' performance was as uneven as its history. Technological tracking and surveillance methods put Americans on the verge of a new quarantinist tradition of authoritarian control. Death rates betrayed glaring inequities in the quality of care in our poor and disenfranchised communities. Triaging policies threatened to reaffirm past discriminations.

But it doesn't have to be this way. We can recommit to a liberal sanitationist tradition. We can use epidemics as occasions for addressing the glaring inequities they illuminate. We can level up rather than down. The choice

—

is ours. We can proceed intelligently into our unsettling future – but only if we grasp where we have been in our often disturbing past.

Chapter 1

THE SANITATIONIST STATE

One of the most deeply engrained legends of American history is that the United States has consistently championed individual freedom over collective solidarity. But early American responses to epidemics exerted considerable state authority and substantially limited individual freedoms in order to achieve great public health victories. Sometimes those victories even became occasions for improving the lives of the poorest among us.

Illness, disease, and death were part of daily life both in the colonies and in the era of the early republic. Smallpox killed far more people during the War for Independence than were killed in battle, partly because the virus came home with soldiers and wreaked havoc in communities all across the new country.[1] Smallpox outbreaks in the Civil War and its aftermath devastated communities of formerly enslaved people.[2] Regular cycles of yellow fever coursed through Charleston, New Orleans, and Savannah. Refugees from revolution in Haiti brought the disease to Philadelphia in 1793, where it killed one in ten residents, and to New York two years later.[3] Hot summers encouraged mosquitoes and led to regular recurrences of the disease in the Northeast for another decade. New Orleans seemed to hardly have a year without cases of yellow fever; outbreaks in the city in the 1850s cost tens of thousands of lives.[4] Cholera reached the United States in 1832, then returned in 1849 and 1866, killing thousands of people in the most gruesome fashion: diarrhea, vomiting, and cramps caused dehydration so severe that sufferers' skin tightened and turned blue from extreme loss of fluids.[5] Many died within hours of their first symptom.

Under such circumstances, pursuing happiness meant promoting health. Early American lawmakers had little understanding of the science of disease – germ theory would not arrive until the United States' second century — but physicians and jurists understood enough to know that infectious disease was a public problem that required collective solutions.

Robust legal authority for responding to public health crises existed from the earliest days of settler colonialism in North America. Scholars have long cited British philosopher John Locke as an originator of the modern tradition of individual freedoms in the liberal state. But Locke's "Fundamental Constitutions," written in 1669 for the colony of Carolina, established a broad power to take care of all "corruption or infection of the common air or water, and all things" necessary to protect "the public commerce and health."[6] Authorities could conscript private property and drain privately owned wetlands. Colonial legal codes regularly made provision to close the courts in the event of pestilence.[7] Such shutdowns were a big deal in an era when court sessions functioned like fair days and served as occasions for auctions and public markets. The colony of Connecticut (like many other colonies) authorized the town officials to isolate and care for any person "visited with the Small Pox" or "suspected to be infected" — and to charge the person or their parents or master for the costs, if possible.[8] In 1761, the colony prohibited smallpox inoculations for fear that they would accidentally spread the disease.

In the early republic, state legislatures and elected officials routinely enacted formidable measures to guard against disease. Six months after the end of the Revolutionary War, the New York legislature empowered the state's governor to set up quarantines to prevent the arrival of yellow fever "or any other contagious Distemper."[9] Within a few years, state officials had built a detailed system of regulations with precise mandates for the loading and unloading of vessels and reporting obligations for boardinghouses, inns, and physicians who became aware of "pestilential or infectious disease" among their guests or patients.[10] New York prohibited importation of cotton or hides between May and November and extended discretionary authority to mayors and to the governor so that they would be empowered to respond quickly to crises.

Early legal provisions against pestilence were state law, partly because the federal government under the weak Articles of Confederation utterly lacked the capacity to act. But the ratification of the new federal Constitution in 1788 did not change matters much, at least with regard to the legal power to regulate the risk of infectious disease. State law remained primary. After a 1793 outbreak of yellow fever, for example, Pennsylvania established a state health office to protect Philadelphia "from the introduction of pestilential and contagious diseases."[11] (The prescient statute incorporating the city just a few years before had listed the "advancement of public health" second only to "the suppression of vice and immorality" among the purposes of the city government.)[12] The city's board of health was empowered to declare private lanes, courts, or alleys a nuisance and to require owners to pave them. Health officials on the Delaware River boasted vast authority over the inspection and quarantining of vessels. Officials themselves were regulated, too. Philadelphia Health Office inspectors were to be fined $20 if they refused to perform their office.

All across the country, states and cities prohibited the burial of bodies in urban settings, ruling out time-honored graveyards in churchyards and public squares and moving interments out to new cemeteries like Green-Wood Cemetery in Brooklyn, Mount Auburn outside Cambridge, Laurel Hill in Philadelphia, and Grove Street in New Haven.

Officials enacted innumerable public health mandates, typically without much fuss. In 1795, Virginia authorized quarantines at "any place within this commonwealth" that "shall become infected with a malignant distemper."[13] Mississippi (like a number of other states) made special provision for removing prisoners when disease broke out in jails.[14] Michigan's first enactments included the creation of local boards empowered to order the removal of "all nuisances, sources of filth, and causes of sickness," including sick people themselves, "that may in their opinion be injurious to the health of the inhabitants within their township."[15] The local Michigan boards had broad authority to restrict the movement and activity of the families of people who had fallen ill. State law even imposed a general obligation on family members to report cases of smallpox among relatives. Failure to report a loved one to the authorities could result in a $100 fine.

As time went by, state and local governments asserted ever more public health powers, and even created new urban administration agencies with broad authority to support public health. In 1827, Boston required that any child attending school be vaccinated against smallpox. Six years later, a tiny new Illinois town called Chicago enacted sweeping sanitary provisions to fend off cholera, including street cleaning, removal of nuisances, banning animal carcass disposal in the river, and regulating the disposal of waste.[16] Urban sanitary codes swelled, embodying a social philosophy of solidarity. "No family, no person liveth to himself alone," declared Massachusetts's 1850 Sanitary Commission. "Every person has a direct or indirect interest in every other person. We are social beings — bound together by indissoluble ties." As the commissioners put it, their work reflected Cicero's ancient legal dictum, *salus populi suprema lex,* to protect one set of human beings from being the victims of disease and death through the selfish cupidity of others."[17]

In early 1866, in anticipation of the coming summer cholera season, and in view of the worsening filth of the streets in the nation's largest city, the New York State legislature established a new Metropolitan Board of Health for Manhattan and the immediate surrounding counties.[18] The legislature endowed the board with the consolidated public health authority of all the local boards of health and the public officials of the city. The commissioners earned salaries, and were authorized to rent offices and to build a staff of attorneys and clerks. They could condemn buildings and machinery and direct the police to carry out their orders, including arresting those who refused to comply, and they could charge the costs of any enforcement proceedings to the property owners. In the event of "great and imminent peril to the public health," the Metropolitan Board had the "extraordinary power" and indeed the duty to take what measures the commissioners believed were warranted, even if not expressly authorized by the legislature.[19]

So vast was the power of the Metropolitan Board, at least by nineteenth-century standards, that the legislature in Albany added one last provision to the law in hopes of protecting the people of New York from an anticipated abuse. It would be a crime to impersonate an officer of the board, punishable by not less than one year in prison.

Of course, the fact that government has the power to do something in theory does not always mean that it can exercise such power effectively in practice. As law-yer-historian Hendrik Hartog shows in a classic study, early New York City struggled for decades to regulate the pigs that wandered in its streets. Enactment after enactment failed to accomplish the goal of clearing the streets of pigs and the refuse they left. Only in 1849, after thirty years of efforts, did city authorities finally remove thou-sands of pigs to fend off a renewed wave of cholera.[20]

* * *

Courts in the early republic almost universally upheld the government's authority to manage the spread of infectious disease. Federal courts upheld quarantines and the detention of vessels at the nation's ports.[21] State courts did, too: in Georgia, the Superior Court upheld a fine levied by Augusta when the owner of a vessel from smallpox-ridden Charleston refused to follow the city council's quarantine rules.[22] In Pennsylvania, the Supreme Court upheld new taxes to procure water sup-plies conducive to the public health.[23] The North Carolina courts upheld a conviction for selling unwholesome meat on the ground that "the public health, whether affected

sodes of a "dreadful epidemic."[27] The Alabama Supreme Court captured the spirit of the law when it voiced Cicero's dictum to uphold the condemnation of two filthy tenements: "Salus populi suprema lex."[28]

Two of the most important cases arose out of New York in the years when the new Erie Canal was causing the city to grow by leaps and bounds. *Brick Presbyterian Church v. Mayor of New York* (1826) arose out of a new regulation prohibiting the interment of bodies in Lower Manhattan.[29] As the historian William Novak has observed, the law "summarily abolished the vested rights" of churches that had been granted permission to use their land for church houses and graveyards.[30] Even more strikingly, the vested rights in question belonged to the leading churches of the city, long powerful brokers in the political marketplace. Yet the New York Supreme Court upheld the new regulation against the churches' challenge, ruling that the cemetery regulation was a "salutary application of police powers," not an unconstitutional taking of property. A year later the same court reaffirmed and extended the point, ruling that the city could prohibit "nuisances to public health" like the church graveyards without paying compensation and without causing "an unconstitutional impairment of the obligation of contracts."[31] Nine years after that, the New York courts upheld the destruction of unsanitary real property to slow a cholera outbreak that had already killed some five hundred people in the city.[32]

In 1868, the early American cases culminated in a decision by the high court of New York State affirming the authority of the new Metropolitan Board of Health. "From the earliest organization of the government," ruled Chief Judge Ward Hunt, states had vested local boards and their officers with "the absolute control over persons and property, so far as the public health was concerned." Hunt, who would soon accept appointment to the U.S. Supreme Court, explained that boards had long "exercised a summary jurisdiction over the subject," which had allowed them to act first and get the approval of the courts later. A dissenter objected that the new Metropolitan Board impermissibly mixed legislative, executive, and judicial power. His complaint anticipated future critiques of the administrative state in the twentieth century. But Hunt and the majority disagreed. The public health powers of the state, he ruled, "were not bound to wait the slow course of the law."[33]

* * *

In the nineteenth century, public health law was so vital that a now mostly forgotten field of law grew up around the problem of disease. "The jurisprudence of hygiene" or "sanitary jurisprudence" took up questions of public health.[34] As early as 1819, Americans were reprinting English authorities on the public health law of contagious diseases.[35] Writers cited the precedent of quarantines from Leviticus.[36] Some medical jurists advised cities to take forceful action to stop the spread of disease.[37] Officials, they advised, should create quarantine lines "not to be transgressed by the infected, nor by the healthy."[38] Authorities were to separate ill family members from healthy ones, forcibly if necessary.

This seemingly arcane field of the law soon became a forum for political debate over the meaning of responsible citizenship. In one respect, the jurisprudence of hygiene contained the seeds of a deep and abiding social reform. When the Massachusetts sanitary commissioners insisted that "no person liveth to himself alone," and that "we are social beings," they were giving voice to values of social interdependence and solidarity.[39] If social conditions and poor urban environs were the determinants of disease, then improving the living conditions of the poor was the way to fight off illness.

John Billings, a U.S. Army surgeon and lecturer on the law of hygiene, embraced this model of sanitary jurisprudence, which we might call a progressive sanitationism. Billings observed in 1879 that people "can have but little power as individuals to avoid, prevent, or destroy" the causes of epidemics and disease. The causes of illness, he insisted, are established for us, not by us. Hygiene, for Billings, was the collective practice of protecting the health of every member of the community. Just as the state protected our liberty and property, so too the state protected our health. Indeed, Billings affirmed the view of Chief Justice John Marshall and Chief Judge Lemuel Shaw in Massachusetts. Liberty and property would sometimes have to give way to public health imperatives. The public's health highlighted the value of collective action through the state, because our incapacity to manage our own environments individually meant that in the domain of public health we are all dependent on government to act for us. In dense cities like New York and Philadelphia, those most at risk of illness posed a risk to everyone else. As Billings put it, the "dangerous classes" were "an ever-present menace."[40]

If the condition of the so-called dangerous classes could be improved, however, the menace of contagion could be managed and even reduced. As one European observer put it, "It is not quarantines, but the rule of law and a chicken in every pot that cholera will respect."[41] Public health was a product of the accumulated social relations and systems of the society. And so, for some, the law of public health turned attention to improving the lives of the poorest Americans. John Griscom, an early sanitarian in New York, observed that a disproportionate share of disease victims were poor immigrants, although the rich seemed to live in ways that were just as profligate and immoderate. Griscom concluded that the bad health and shorter life spans of the city's immigrant populations were due to "the confined spaces in which they dwell, the unwholesome air they breathe, and their filth and degradation."[42] In 1867, New York adopted a new tenement housing code that increased tenants' standard of living by mandating a minimum of one privy per twenty tenement inhabitants; a few years later the state upped the minimum to one per fifteen.[43]

In the early twentieth century, Progressive reformers worked to further improve the conditions of poor urban dwellers. New York enacted a series of laws regulating tenements. Child health stations offered infants safe milk and vaccines for smallpox and diphtheria.[44] Reformer Lillian Wald founded the Visiting Nurse Service at her Henry Street Settlement and led efforts to fight tuberculosis and other infectious diseases in immigrant communities.[45] Wald's colleague Florence Kelley headed the National Consumers League, which drew attention to the risks of unsanitary conditions for workers, in part by observing that such conditions posed dangers for middle-class consumers of the goods such workers produced.[46] (Consumers, she warned, might be "buying smallpox.")[47] Some, like the American Medical Association, focused on the personal habits of the working poor, blaming them for spitting in the streets and on floors. But

Progressives such as Kelley and Wald scoffed that such a focus obscured the real issues. "Everybody knows the true remedy," wrote the novelist and political agitator Upton Sinclair, "which would be the paying of sufficient wages, and the tearing down of the filthy tenements into which the laborers are packed."[48]

At other times, and in other hands, however, the jurisprudence of hygiene could produce a politics that focused on individual rather than social responsibility. In London, public health reformer Edwin Chadwick epitomized the conservative version of sanitationism.[49] Chadwick was a leading force behind the 1834 reforms to the British Poor Laws, which aimed to reduce the costs of poor relief by instituting draconian workhouses and pushing people back into the labor force. By the 1840s, he was, in one biographer's estimation, "the most unpopular single individual in the whole kingdom," and for good reason.[50] Chadwick was a standoffish and prickly character. In his view, attention to the public health of the poor and the working classes would produce better habits of thrift, temperance, and hard work. Filth produced moral decay, Chadwick insisted, and his massive 1842

—

Report on the Sanitary Condition of the Labouring Population of Great Britain advocated cleanliness — better sanitation, water, and sewage services — as a way of further reducing the costs of poor relief and improving the labor supply to British industry.[51]

Here was a very different politics of sanitation, not a progressive view that might lead to bettering the conditions of the poor, but a conservative or reactionary view that saw sanitation as a path to maximizing the value of the laboring poor and protecting elites from the risks of contagions spilling out of poor neighborhoods. In the United States, mid-nineteenth-century sanitarians like Massachusetts's Lemuel Shattuck carried Chadwick's view forward, imagining that poor health and poor hygiene were signs of a lack of moral virtue. States like Michigan in 1899 made it a crime for people with venereal disease (along with epileptics and the supposedly feebleminded) to exercise the right to marry.[52] In myriad ways, the poor and disadvantaged were blamed for their bad health — and not only for their own. In the 1916 polio epidemic, rates of the disease were higher in wealthy neighborhoods, at least in part because improved sanitation in middle- and upper-class homes deprived young children of early exposure to the polio virus, leaving them without the usual levels of immunity. Yet public health authorities focused nonetheless on the supposed dangerous filth of poor neighborhoods. Quarantine requirements for polio epidemics, moreover, were often regressive, needlessly imposing impractical mandates for separate dining and toilet facilities. "No tenement dweller," writes the polio historian Naomi Rogers, "could have complied."[53]

* * *

Sanitationism's two political valences — one progressive, the other conservative — competed with one another throughout the nineteenth and into the twentieth century. Still, the progressive and conservative variants of sanitationism typically shared a common aim. They took the welfare of the poor and the working class seriously, even if they arrived at different prescriptions. They were both, at their core, forms of liberal politics.

The structure of American government was relatively well suited to pursuing both forms of nineteenth-century sanitationism. The federal government, with its limited constitutional authority, played virtually no role. But state and local governments were able to promote sanitationist strategies for disease control. Thanks to the slow speed of transportation relative to later eras, the scope of eighteenth- and nineteenth-century epidemics often more or less matched the capacity of state and local jurisdictions.[54] Expensive local and state investments in public health would serve the interests of local taxpayers, who benefited in the form of reduced risks of disease. Public health problems, as John Billings had observed, could align the interests of middle- and upper-class taxpayers with the poor and the working class, at least to a degree.

Yet the capacities of the American state were poorly designed to achieve the more ambitiously progressive sanitationist visions. State and local governments were informal and underfunded affairs, run by amateur statesmen. This was not all bad; amateur hour in the statehouse has made it harder for certain tyrannical forms of statecraft to emerge. But a different and more authoritarian story line developed when the interests of those with power and those without were no longer aligned.

Chapter 2

QUARANTINISM IN AMERICA

In 1793, shortly after the second inauguration of President George Washington, and while the federal government still resided in Philadelphia, yellow fever raced through the City of Brotherly Love.[1] People with the means fled to the countryside; Washington himself escaped to the bucolic suburb of Germantown. Of those who stayed behind, nearly half — some seventeen thousand people — fell ill, and five thousand died. Faced with the question of how to allocate the labor of caring for the ill and burying the dead, the town fathers, who six years earlier had presided over the drafting of the U.S. Constitution, hit upon an idea that would shield them and their families from risk. They recklessly asserted that the city's

—

small Black population was immune to the disease and called on the Black community to do the ghastly work. Hundreds of African Americans died before the outbreak passed.[2] Those who survived were scapegoated for taking payments for their services and even accused of theft from the homes of the sick.

If the American law of epidemics has had a liberal *sanitationist* thread focused on protecting citizens' health and improving their living conditions, it has also contained an equally important *quarantinist* side, exerting authoritarian and discriminatory control over people of color, the poor, and immigrant newcomers.

* * *

Quarantines in North American ports go back to the seventeenth century. The Massachusetts Bay Colony established a quarantine for vessels from Barbados when yellow fever broke out there in 1647. The port colonies along the eastern seaboard each enacted elaborate systems of quarantine, inspection, and cleaning for inbound vessels, violation of which was punished as a crime. In an age in which most goods were imported, this was no small imposition on daily life and constrained the freedoms of both those on ship and those awaiting a vessel on land.

By the nineteenth century, quarantine rules in the nation's major ports regulated vessels, their cargo, and their crews in minute detail. In New Orleans, for example, the port required disclosure of detailed information not only about the cargo but about the origins and health of all on board; in New York, the city health department controlled the unloading of goods and passengers; in Philadelphia, the port inspector stopped all incoming traffic at an island in the Delaware River some miles downstream of the city.

Quarantines at the nation's ports shaped the commerce of the era, and they offered at least some protection against the introduction of disease from remote places. Politically, they were made easier by the simple fact that their principal targets had little claim to be represented in local politics. On land, by contrast, quarantines, detentions, and other heavy-handed acts of state authority produced far more controversy because they affected citizens and residents, though they tended to discriminate against people who, for reasons of race, ethnicity, and class, had little power over their political fortunes.

* * *

The first land-based quarantine in the history of colonial North America may have come in East Hampton, Long Island, where two and a half centuries later rich financiers would shelter during another pandemic. On March 2, 1662, town authorities "ordered that no Indian shall come to towne . . . until they be free of the small poxe," nor "any English or Indian servant go to their wigwams," on pain of being fined and whipped.[3]

Thus commenced one strand in a long and ugly tradition of heavy-handed government action and indifferent neglect by which colonial authorities and later the United States would entrench racial, ethnic, and class inequalities. Government authorities left Native Americans to suffer from infectious disease without help on countless occasions. Military officials deliberately spread disease among Native Americans by sending them infected materials.[4] The myth of Black immunity to yellow fever put African Americans at risk up and down the eastern seaboard in the late eighteenth century. In places like New Orleans, where yellow fever was endemic, enslaved people who had survived the fever developed what historian Kathryn Olivarius calls "immunocapital": their owners were rewarded by the enhanced value that immunity delivered.[5]

Public health authorities often targeted immigrant and minority communities for enforcement. Pennsylvania's 1794 law creating a health office in the wake of the yellow fever outbreak, for example, was subtitled "An Act . . . for Regulating the Importation of German and Other Passengers."[6] When cholera arrived in the middle of the nineteenth century, Irish Catholics often accused public health officials of targeting their communities for property condemnation and other aggressive measures. Tens of thousands of freedpeople died when a smallpox epidemic ravaged the refugee camps nominally managed by the War Department.[7] As historian Tera Hunter notes, one missionary reported seeing dying victims "lying on the damp ground suffering in every degree."[8] For far too many, the dislocation and desperation resulting from the Civil War and emancipation, together with the indifference of the government, led to infection, disfigurement, blindness, or death.

Throughout the nineteenth century, authorities mandated risky vaccinations for poor and disenfranchised populations, the "prowling negroes and shabby whites," as a New Orleans sanitary inspector called them in 1877.[9] By the turn of the century, urban officials blamed new arrivals from southern and eastern Europe for bringing disease and infection. When a vessel carrying Russian Jewish immigrants was linked to a typhus outbreak in 1892, for example, New York authorities quarantined all entering Russian Jews, without regard to their individual circumstances.[10] Discriminatory state power was sometimes exercised against specific individuals as well as against particular communities. Consider Mary Mallon, dubbed "Typhoid Mary," whose sad life story offers an especially vivid illustration.[11] Mallon was an unmarried, middle-aged, Irish-born domestic cook in Manhattan in 1907 when outbreaks of typhoid fever occurred among several of Manhattan's wealthiest households. An enterprising public health official traced the outbreaks back to Mallon, who had served in each of the affected households. Mallon had experienced no symptoms. She was not sick in any conventional sense. Nor had she done anything wrong. She had certainly committed no crime. Yet the board of health and the New York City police seized her. Testing soon revealed that she was a healthy carrier of the typhoid bacillus, and she was detained in quarantine on North Brother Island in the East River. A New York judge upheld her detention as lawful under the powers of the Metropolitan Board of Health. After almost three years of isolation, she was released on a promise never to work as a cook again. But she did not believe the science. Taking an assumed name, she went to work as a cook for a maternity ward. She was discovered in 1915 when typhoid fever broke out in the ward and investigators traced the disease back to her. She would spend the rest of her life, twenty-three years, once again isolated against her will in the East River, never having been convicted of or even charged with a crime. Several hundred other healthy carriers of the bacillus came to light while Mallon moldered alone on North Brother Island, but none was detained for a substantial period of time.

In part, Mallon's special treatment resulted from her defiance of public health mandates. But as biographer Judith Walzer Leavitt contends, Mallon also fell victim to an array of prejudices. She was poor and Irish and unmarried. To some, such traits made her seem unworthy of personal freedom.

* * *

People of color and other minorities have been especially vulnerable to discrimination in the law of epidemics. In March 1900, a suspected death from bubonic plague in San Francisco led to an immediate lockdown of the city's Chinatown, with an order that no one be permitted to cross the quarantine line except white people, who were allowed out.[12] San Francisco's board of health issued a further order requiring every Chinese person in the city—and only every Chinese person—to undergo a dangerous inoculation. The plague had caused millions of deaths in the previous decade in India and East Asia, so considering Chinatown a place of particular risk may not have been irrational. But the board of health did not recognize that the heightened risk was a product of the discrimination that led Chinese residents to be concentrated in one neighborhood in the first place. The race specificity of the city's response made clear, too, that reinforcing racial hierarchies was at least as important as public health imperatives.

In 1924, another outbreak of bubonic plague, this time in Los Angeles, killed forty people, most of them of Mexican descent. City authorities roped off Mexican neighborhoods and forbade entrance or exit. Squads of quickly deputized white Angelenos moved through the quarantined neighborhoods, destroying property, laying rat traps, and spraying disinfectant. Some twenty-five hundred buildings were condemned as nuisances and destroyed, most of them homes for Mexican and Mexican American families and workers. The city offered no compensation, reasoning that the homes had been public nuisances and a source of pestilence and infection. Nor did city officials move to construct new housing. Instead, as the city's Bureau of Housing and Sanitation candidly conceded, the former residents had been scattered to houses and quarters so unfit for habitation as to be "a barrier to the progress of the life and character of the persons living in them." Historian William Deverell calls the entire episode "a Southern California experiment with ethnic cleansing."[13]

For African American communities, the malign indifference and contempt shown by the law of public health lasted long past the 1793 yellow fever outbreak in Philadelphia. When smallpox broke out in Washington, D.C., in 1862, the Medical Division of the Freedmen's Bureau blamed freedpeople. Healthy and infected freedpeople alike were forced into crowded, unsanitary prisons and tented communities, where disease raced through the population. In the early twentieth century, the city council of Macon, Georgia, passed an ordinance requiring that Black servants register and show that they were disease free in order to qualify for a mandatory license or "badge," which some compared to the tags supplied for properly vaccinated dogs.[14] In Atlanta, police raided the homes of Black laundresses unfairly suspected of spreading disease to white households. In the middle of the century in cities like Baltimore, urban renewal authorities singled out Black neighborhoods as sources of tuberculosis, thus legitimating the condemnation of entire blocks to make way for highways and parks that often served more affluent communities.

One of the most stunning episodes of white supremacy in American statecraft arose when government scientists chose to treat Black men as test subjects in an experiment to learn about the course of infectious diseases in the human body.[15] In 1932, at the height of the Great Depression, philanthropic funding ran out for an ongoing study of syphilis in Black men in Tuskegee, Alabama. Officials at the U.S. Public Health Service decided to take the opportunity to experiment on some four hundred Black men with confirmed latent syphilis to see what effect the disease would have if left untreated. For forty years, doctors concocted elaborate lies, assuring patients they were being cared for. Their real aim was to perform autopsies on the study's victims to be able to learn more about syphilis. The study's white leaders understood that they were shortening the lives and contributing to the ailments of the study's subjects by withholding care. Only in 1972, when a whistleblower leaked information to the press, did the government halt the program.

The emergence of HIV/AIDS in the 1980s revealed further biases in the government's and the law's response to infectious disease.[16] For six years after the onset of the epidemic, which was known to infect primarily sexually active gay men, President Ronald Reagan refused even to say the word *AIDS* in public. Only after more than twenty thousand Americans had died and only after unrelenting pressure from activists did Reagan ask his surgeon general, Dr. C. Everett Koop, to draft a report on the disease. Senior administration officials battled to prevent Koop from being candid about safer-sex practices, such as condom use and mutual masturbation, that would help combat the illness's spread. Meanwhile, Senator Jesse Helms of North Carolina denounced gay men as "perverts" on the floor of the Senate and sponsored an amendment to an appropriations bill that prohibited the use of federal funds in ways deemed to "promote or encourage" homosexual sex.[17] The Senate passed the gag order of the Helms Amendment by a resounding vote of 96-2.

The AIDS crisis coincided with an unprecedented rise in incarceration as the criminal justice system's response to crime and drugs. Between the 1960s and the end of the 1980s the prison population quadrupled to some eight hundred thousand persons, a disproportionate number of them poor African Americans or Latinx. Unprotected sex and illicit drug use in prisons made these institutions foci of infection, which then spread into communities upon the inmates' release. Legal prohibitions on sex education combined with mass incarceration helped lead to 774,467 infections and 448,060 deaths by the end of the 1990s.[18]

***

The quarantinist impulse has always been apparent in the law of immigration and border control. For the first hundred years of the American republic, as scholars Hidetaka Hirota and Gerald Neuman have shown, immigration law was state law, not federal.[19] Eighteenth-century officials in places like Massachusetts and New York were empowered to expel persons newly arrived from areas thought to have smallpox or other diseases.[20] Virtually every coastal state authorized the forcible detention and isolation of immigrants to stop the spread of disease, and states typically vested port officials with broad powers of inspection and detention, often requiring that vessels present a clean bill of health signed by officials from the vessel's port of embarkation.[21] State quarantines regularly carried with them prejudices against poor immigrants and nonwhite immigrants.[22] In the 1880s and 1890s, for example, the San Francisco Board of Health targeted vessels from Asian ports for special inspection and disinfection rules.[23] The city made all passengers on such vessels subject to inspection, but only passengers of Asian descent were also subject to arbitrary detention.

State public health controls produced jail-like detentions for hundreds of thousands, if not millions, of would-be immigrants suspected of carrying disease. In 1799, New York established a large quarantine facility known as the Marine Hospital on Staten Island, to which port officials sent vessels, passengers, and cargo suspected of infection. For six decades, would-be newcomers found themselves forcibly confined in the Marine Hospital — until anxious Staten Island residents burned the facility to the ground in 1858 to keep infection away from the island.[24] (The *New York Times* called it the "Battle of Staten Island" and denounced the arsonists as a mob; a jury saw the episode differently and acquitted those charged with crimes.) After the fire, the state built new quarantine buildings on Hoffman Island and the smaller Swinburne Island in New York Harbor, just on the ocean side of where the Verrazano-Narrows Bridge now stands. Photographs from the early twentieth century show crowds of immigrants detained on the islands, housed in barracks and penned in by chain-link fence and armed guards.

On the West Coast, new arrivals often found themselves inspected and detained in San Francisco Harbor, first in a dismal detention shed run by the Pacific Mail Steamship Company, and then, beginning in 1910, at the federal facility at Angel Island.[25] Approximately three hundred thousand people were held at Angel Island between 1910 and 1940.[26] Most were Asian, largely from China with a smaller number from Japan, and many found themselves held in the facility's health quarantine system for days or even months.

The federal role at Angel Island was no anomaly. The federal government has been especially active in the management of infectious diseases in the ports and at the borders, though federal law got a slow start compared to state law. As early as the 1790s, Congress debated enacting federal quarantine rules in U.S. ports. But critics of the idea successfully argued that the ports were better managed by the states. Defenders of state sovereignty even managed to turn early federal immigration debates into occasions for strengthening state-level health and quarantine laws. In 1796, Congress enacted a law authorizing the president to aid in the execution of state quarantines and health laws.[27] Three years later, Congress mandated that federal revenue officials provide such aid.[28] However, not even the waves of cholera epidemics in the middle of the nineteenth century could change the basic fact of state and local authority in the ports.[29] At the end of the nineteenth century, in 1893, Congress started regulating quarantines more forcibly, setting minimum standards for state quarantine laws.[30] One by one, states turned over quarantine power to the federal government. In 1921, New York became the last state to do so.

Federal immigration and border controls targeting infectious disease have discriminated on the basis of race and ethnicity since the very beginnings of federal involvement. Proponents of the Chinese Exclusion Act, passed by Congress in 1882, relied heavily on the supposed filth and disease of Chinese immigrants as grounds for the law. (This despite evidence from congressional hearings that Chinese immigrants as a class were substantially healthier than whites.)[31] A decade later, the Alien Labor Immigration Act of 1891 barred "persons suffering from a loathsome or a dangerous contagious disease" from admission to the United States, along with "all idiots, insane persons, paupers, or persons likely to become a public charge."[32] After World War I, nativist anti-immigration sentiment focused even more attention on the supposed dangers of infectious diseases among immigrants. The *New York Times* sneered at newcomers from eastern and southern Europe who brought "loathsome diseases of the flesh" alongside ideological infections like "ignorance and Bolshevism."[33] Others objected to immigrants from Latin America, who were said to be "rotten with various diseases." In 1924, such concerns helped bring an end to the era of mass European immigration, imposing narrow national quotas designed to solidify the country's supposed (though largely imagined) Anglo-Saxon demographics.

On the southern border, U.S. border officials established a cordon sanitaire that reflected and reproduced race
and class divisions. Beginning with a yellow fever outbreak
in 1882, U.S. border officers began enforcing aggressive
health measures at the Texas-Mexico border. For the next
three-quarters of a century, public health officials subjected
laborers to humiliating and often arbitrary and capricious
regimens of inspections, detentions, and washing. Workers in the Bracero program, for example, which brought
Mexican farm laborers into the country for seasonal
work between 1942 and 1964, were regularly stripped
and deloused with harsh, noxious chemicals sprayed on
their faces and genitals.[34] The U.S. Public Health Service,
remembered one Mexican migrant, "disinfected us as if
we were some kind of animals." It "was discrimination,
and it was not right," remembered another.[35] Historians
John Mckiernan-González and Alexandra Minna Stern
have shown that the application of forceful public health
measures on the southern border helped to sustain the
pernicious racial science of the early twentieth century.[36]

New forms of imperialism projected the American
law of public health beyond the border, too. Sometimes

—

this had happy effects. New attention to yellow fever by American doctors during the U.S. occupation of Cuba after 1898 helped to confirm the theory (first developed by a Cuban physician named Carlos Finlay in 1881) that mosquitoes transmitted the disease.[37] In building the Panama Canal between 1904 and 1914, the U.S.-controlled Isthmian Canal Commission (ICC) and the U.S. Public Health Service combined to radically reduce deaths from malaria and yellow fever. But American officials exercising power abroad often did so in a way that reinforced racial status hierarchies. The ICC housed highly paid white workers in homes with mosquito screens and provided them high-quality health care. Black laborers from Barbados and Jamaica, by contrast, had to make do with tents without screens in mosquito-filled areas. Their death rates were at least four times those of white workers. Efforts to fight disease in the area even took the form of a kind of racial zoning. The ICC's sanitary department, run by American military physician William Gorgas, dictated that buildings for ICC officials and white Americans be placed at least one thousand feet from the "native huts" of local Panamanians.[38]

* * *

Courts made clear from early in the history of the United States that states and the federal government had broad, and often concurrent, power to establish quarantines and other forceful health measures at the border. State courts uniformly supported state government authority to implement quarantines and public health regulations in port cities, without the complex balancing of state and federal authority. In *DuBois v. Augusta,* for example, decided in 1831, the Georgia Supreme Court defended quarantine regulations as "necessary for the security, welfare and convenience" of the people. The court explicitly rebuked those who would break such quarantine regulations: "The safety of the whole community," the court warned, "is not to be hazarded upon the speculations of any captain of a boat."[39]

In 1837, the justices of the U.S. Supreme Court affirmed this general power in a case challenging New York's requirement that arriving vessels submit reports on their passengers' names, origins, and occupations. Public health authority served as the basis for powers such as those asserted in the New York regulation. "On the same principle by which a state may prevent the introduction of infected persons or goods," Justice Henry Baldwin explained, "it may exclude paupers who will add to the burdens of taxation."[40]

A decade later, in a pair of disputes known as the *Passenger Cases,* a splintered Court preserved the authority of the states even as it voted 5-4 to strike down a New York statute authorizing the state health commissioner to collect a tax on passengers arriving in the state's ports.[41] The law in question established a head tax for vessels from foreign ports of $1 for every steerage passenger and member of the crew, and $1.50 for every master or cabin passenger; for vessels from coastal ports of the United States, the law created a simple tax of 25 cents for each passenger, with a discount for vessels from nearby states. Most of the money went to support the Marine Hospital on Staten Island. Five justices voted to strike down the law as an unconstitutional regulation of interstate and international commerce, which the justices in the majority ruled was reserved to the Congress. The case was caught up in a raging controversy about states' authority to exclude Black people. (Chief Justice Roger Taney, who would later draft the opinion in the infamous *Dred Scott* case, voted to uphold states' authority to tax and exclude newcomers.) In the 1860s, the Civil War and the Fourteenth Amendment would resolve the question about whether states could formally exclude Blacks. But in the meanwhile, all the justices reaffirmed that state health laws at the nation's ports remained valid. Justice John McLean, writing in the majority, reassured states that they could continue to "guard against the introduction of any thing which may corrupt the morals, or endanger the health or lives of their citizens."[42] Following Justice McLean's hint, New York promptly circumvented the Court's decision. The state enacted a draconian bonding requirement of $300 for each immigrant arriving in its ports to account for the risk the immigrant would become a public charge on the state. A passenger could avoid the bond by payment of a comparatively small fee of $1.50, which almost all passengers preferred to pay. With a few creative strokes of a pen, New York's legislature re-created the immigrant health tax the Court had struck down. The new law would survive for the next quarter century.[43]

—

The U.S. Supreme Court's most important role in the law of public health at the border, however, has undoubtedly been its establishment of the doctrine of plenary congressional power. In a series of cases upholding the Chinese exclusion policies inaugurated in the 1882 Chinese Exclusion Act, the Court established what would later be called the "plenary power" of the federal government over questions of immigration—an essentially unrestricted power derived from the international law of what it is to be a nation-state.[44] The public health authority to exclude infectious persons, explained the Court in its 1889 decision *Chae Chan Ping v. United States,* was at the root of the federal power in question; the "exclusion of paupers, criminals, and persons afflicted with incurable diseases," wrote Justice Stephen Field, "is only an application of the same power to particular classes of persons, whose presence is deemed injurious or a source of danger to the country."[45]

By the early twentieth century, the Supreme Court recognized a similarly awesome power in the authority of states to mandate vaccinations against epidemic diseases. *Jacobson v. Massachusetts,* decided in 1905, was arguably one of the most expansive authorizations of the state's coercive force in American history. Three years earlier, the Cambridge Board of Health had ordered that all adults be vaccinated for smallpox, with no exceptions, at pain of a $5 fine. But Pastor Henning Jacobson, a forty-five-year-old husband, father of three, immigrant from Sweden, and pastor of a local Lutheran church, refused. Even when the board came to his door, he declined. He had experienced bad vaccinations for smallpox twice before, once during his own childhood in Sweden, which he remembered as causing "great and extreme suffering," and a second time when one of his sons was vaccinated in the United States. And so he was willing to face charges for defying the board of health. The state convicted Jacobson, along with three other vaccination resisters, of violating the board of health order. The Massachusetts Supreme Judicial Court affirmed the conviction, and Jacobson appealed to the U.S. Supreme Court, arguing that the state lacked the authority to forcibly inject a dangerous substance into unwilling citizens.

The Court upheld the vaccine mandate in a 7-2 decision. "The police power of a state," Justice John Marshall Harlan wrote, "must be held to embrace, at least, such reasonable regulations established directly by legislative enactments as will protect the public health and the public safety." What Harlan called "real liberty" did not mean the freedom to act as one pleases "regardless of the injury that may be done to others." No, "the liberty secured by the Constitution" did "not import an absolute right in each person to be . . . freed from restraint." To the contrary, Harlan continued, "there are manifold restraints to which every person is necessarily subject for the common good."[46]

As historian Michael Willrich has observed, *Jacobson*'s expansive conception of state authority would form the basis for one of the Supreme Court's lowest moments.[47] In *Buck v. Bell*, decided in 1927, Justice Oliver Wendell Holmes upheld the compulsory sterilization of Carrie Buck, a young Virginia woman who had been wrongly labeled "feebleminded" after becoming pregnant out of wedlock. "The principle that sustains compulsory vaccination is broad enough to cover cutting the Fallopian tubes," Holmes wrote, citing *Jacobson*. "Three generations of imbeciles," Holmes concluded, "are enough."[48]

Yet Justice Harlan's *Jacobson* opinion also contained a recessive note that many observers have failed to observe. A different case might have produced an entirely different result, Harlan explained. The "arbitrary and oppressive" use of vaccination might be unconstitutional. For example, if "a particular condition" of the plaintiff's "health or body" made vaccination "cruel and inhuman," then a court might be "competent to interfere and protect the health and life of the individual concerned."[49] Perhaps Harlan and his colleagues had overlooked the fact that Henning Jacobson had made that very argument. Or maybe Harlan was ensuring judicial oversight in future infectious disease emergencies. Courts reviewing public health programs for constitutional violations have authorized vast government authority—but they have never been willing to get entirely out of the way. Justice Harlan's caveat in *Jacobson* stands as part of a long tradition of channeling, if not exactly checking, the breathtaking powers of the quarantinist state.

Chapter 3

CIVIL LIBERTIES IN AN EPIDEMIC?

At the end of March 2020, Governor Gina Raimondo of Rhode Island faced a dilemma. States all around the small Ocean State were developing serious COVID-19 crises.[1] Connecticut, the state's immediate neighbor, was experiencing a substantial outbreak. Immediately to Connecticut's west, New York had emerged as the nation's early hotspot for the disease. Large numbers of wealthy New Yorkers owned beach homes in Rhode Island. And so Raimondo took decisive action. She deployed National Guard troops to the Connecticut border, where they ordered cars to pull over if they had out-of-state plates. Uniformed soldiers took contact information so that the state's health department could track visitors staying for

—

more than one day. Those entering from out of state were instructed to quarantine themselves for two weeks. Further orders followed, closing certain businesses, requiring that people stay home, and imposing isolation and quarantine mandates on sick and potentially sick people. Opinion polls in the state showed that the governor's popularity had never been higher.[2]

Yet decisive government action in American law usually produces an equal and opposite counterreaction. Critics soon attacked Raimondo for violating individual rights. Governor Andrew Cuomo in New York protested Rhode Island's initial decision to single out New Yorkers.[3] Wasn't that a violation of New Yorkers' right to travel? The local Rhode Island chapter of the American Civil Liberties Union objected that people were being effectively detained "solely for the 'offense' of coming from out of state" without any opportunity to be heard. "We fully appreciate that the state is dealing with an emergency crisis that requires emergency actions," said the chapter's executive director, "but it should not be at the unwarranted expense of our civil rights."[4] Critics emerged on the political right, too. A conservative advocacy group threatened to sue. "Civil liberties, including religious rights, the right to peaceably assemble, the right to earn an honest living, and the right to travel," warned the Rhode Island Center for Freedom and Prosperity, "may have been violated."[5] Raimondo's orders, insisted free-market civil libertarians, amounted to uncompensated takings of private property.

In the end, there was no judicial resolution of the Rhode Island dispute. Conditions changed. The orders lapsed. Courts did not intervene.

But were the critics right? Raimondo answered that as governor she had "a duty to protect the people of Rhode Island."[6] Most Rhode Islanders seem to have agreed. But were there limits to what she could do to protect the health of the state? Or did the rights of travelers on the highways come first?

* * *

If one had to identify the person who first learned how the American legal system would answer such questions, one could do worse than to start with an obscure New York lawyer named George Bliss Jr.[7]

Born in Springfield, Massachusetts, in 1830 to a prosperous family of lawyers, Bliss studied law at Harvard before moving to New York, where he helped organize three so-called colored regiments to fight in the Civil War. In 1872 President Ulysses S. Grant appointed him United States attorney for the Southern District of New York, the most important U.S. attorney posting in the country. But Bliss's most challenging job, by some measures, came right after the war, when he became the attorney for New York's new Metropolitan Board of Health.

By 1866, courts had established a broad authority of the states to regulate to promote the public health of their citizens. A few years later, the U.S. Supreme Court would confirm that this power remained in place even after the new Fourteenth Amendment; in the *Slaughter-House Cases*, the Court upheld a Louisiana health law aiming to keep animal waste out of the water supply. The Metropolitan Board of Health ought, therefore, to have had clear sailing in the exercise of its powers. The opposite quickly proved true. For one thing, the New York legislature had failed to deliver certain crucial powers to the board, at least as Bliss saw it. It had proven cumbersome to collect from property owners the costs incurred by the board in the repair of tenement buildings found not to comply with the sanitary code. Reporting requirements for births, deaths, and marriages were not being enforced. The power to oversee street cleaning and the removal of garbage had not been consolidated under the board, but Bliss thought it indispensable that the board manage the contracts for such services. The board needed "preventative power," too: the authority to order that lots remain clean into the future, not merely the power to sanction landowners whose lots had already fallen into a dangerous condition.

More than anything else, Bliss believed, the board was impeded by the courts. "The courts," he wrote in his first annual report, "have greatly interfered with the execution and the orders of the board." In all, courts issued as many as one thousand injunctions against the board's actions during Bliss's tenure. Judge George Barnard, soon to be impeached for corruption, enjoined the board from removing the stands and stalls around Washington Market at Vesey and West Streets. Similar injunctions barred the board from improving the sanitary conditions of the Fulton Market and the Franklin Market. Another judge forbade the board from issuing cease-and-desist orders to the proprietors of noxious fertilizer businesses in downtown Manhattan. Still others blocked the board from using properties in Staten Island and Coney Island to monitor cholera. (Neighbors had objected, fearing that the board's work would increase the risk of contagion in the surrounding community.) Judges stopped the board from interfering with the rights of commercial fat boilers to make glue and shell burners to make fertilizers. The "operations of the Board," Bliss concluded, "have been cramped and thwarted at every turn."[8]

Even as Bliss reflected on his first year at the board of health, however, the tide was shifting. Courts began to acknowledge that regulating fat boilers was within the board's powers. Judge Joseph Dowling ruled that the law was "a most salutary one, made for the benefit of the poor man."[9] A year later, Bliss could report that the courts, on the whole, had "interfered with the operations of the Board far less during the present year than during the preceding one." Yet Bliss noted a crucial caveat. "Where they decided in our favor," Bliss reported, "they placed

—

their decision, not on the ground that the conclusion of the board was final, but that it was shown by affidavits to be correct."[10] The judges, in other words, had refused to defer to the board on the core questions of the board's competence. Courts were making their own independent judgments on the question of whether a business or a property was a public health nuisance. In doing so, of course, the courts substantially limited the board's power. But that was precisely the point. Civil liberties legal challenges have rarely blocked public health authority altogether. But as Bliss discovered, civil liberties and constitutional protections have shaped the police power over public health, pushing it in new directions, and occasionally even checking its excesses.

★ ★ ★

One source of judicial authority to check public health measures arises out of the complex, many-layered structure of state power in the United States. *People v. Roff,* a case decided by the New York Supreme Court in Kings County in 1856, arose out of a controversy involving the Marine Hospital on Staten Island. Judge Lucien

Birdseye reversed the conviction of a state health official charged with violating a local ordinance prohibiting anyone from passing from the Marine Hospital into other parts of the town of Castleton, in which the hospital was located. "It can never be permitted," wrote Judge Birdseye, "that, even for the sake of the public health, any local, inferior board or tribunal shall repeal statutes, suspend the operation of the constitution, and infringe all the natural rights of the citizen."[11]

In truth, however, Judge Birdseye's ruling was far narrower than his broad language suggested. The problem with the Staten Island regulation was not that it infringed anyone's natural rights or liberty. The difficulty was that the local quarantine ordinance could not be lawful when it conflicted with the state's own public health regulations. The statewide rules out of Albany superseded the local rules of Staten Island.

Judge Birdseye was no outlier. Nineteenth-century courts often struck down state and local public health orders when they concluded that legal authority for them was lacking. In 1858, when the town of Salisbury in western North Carolina moved to enforce an ordinance banning entry into the town by anyone from a place infected with smallpox, the state Supreme Court blocked the town by reading the ordinance narrowly. The ordinance, ruled the court, embraced only those persons leaving an infected place after enactment of the ordinance and traveling directly to the town.[12] A decade later, the Supreme Court of Georgia allowed a suit for damages to go forward by a property owner who objected to local officials' appropriation of his land to build a smallpox hospital; the state code, held the court, authorized local officials to establish such hospitals, but not to seize property to do so.[13] A court in Maine allowed property owners to win damages from state officials who had impressed their property to take smallpox patients to hospitals on the grounds that the public health authority of such officials existed only when expressly granted — and that under enactments of the Maine legislature, it applied only to the isolation of infected goods, not infected people.[14] In principle, each of these cases conceded the authority of towns or states to enact the kinds of public health laws at issue. But each asserted that the relevant body had not yet done so.

—

Courts, as we have seen, generally upheld the authority to impose quarantines at the borders and in the ports. But the quarantine power of local officials was not unbounded. In *Sumner v. Philadelphia*, a federal judge in the Eastern District of Pennsylvania ruled that the state quarantine regulations authorized detention for only so long as reasonably necessary.[15] Rejecting the city's argument that it had absolute, unreviewable discretion in its quarantine decisions, the court awarded damages to the owners of a vessel that had been held in quarantine for some three months.

Similarly, the power to condemn property that threatened public health did not mean an unreviewable or absolute power to decide the fate of such a property. In the 1890s, a case arising out of a particular vermin-infested, darkened five-story tenement ricocheted through the New York courts.[16] The building was located in the interior of a block in the city's Lower East Side and housed 115 people. Conditions were so bad that one-third of children under the age of five living in the building had died between May 1895 and May 1896. The health department had condemned the building and

—

slated it for destruction. But the owner insisted that the department had not been able to show that the building was incapable of being repaired such that it would no longer be a danger to the public health. The courts agreed.

Some judicial decisions seemed to split hairs in their strict construction of state authority. When in 1877 a New York court struck down a health department fine for failure to ventilate a property in accordance with health department orders, it reasoned that the department was authorized to penalize violations of the state sanitary code, but not violations of its own orders pursuant to that code.[17] That same year, the Wisconsin Supreme Court blocked school districts from refusing to admit children without the required smallpox vaccinations on a similar theory; the state board of health, ruled the court, had exceeded its statutory authority when it prohibited nonvaccinated children from attending schools at a time when (in the court's judgment) no smallpox epidemic existed.[18] The high courts of Illinois, Michigan, and Kansas followed suit with more or less similar reasoning.[19] ("In cases of emergency only," reasoned the Minnesota Supreme Court, after a jury had confirmed the public health finding of the local board of school inspectors.)[20] Such decisions gave public health officials headaches. Sometimes they undoubtedly exposed communities to greater risk of contagious diseases. But they also allowed courts to find a middle path by which judges could acknowledge the demands of state emergency powers without having to decide once and for all thorny questions about individual freedom. When narrower technical grounds allowed the courts to resolve disputes over public health powers, as one justice of the Michigan Supreme Court noted, courts did "not feel called upon to enter upon or discuss" the broader questions.[21] By finding technical failures in the public health laws of the state, courts accommodated both state power and individual liberty.

Even when courts upheld programs such as compulsory vaccination, they often clarified that permission was not a blank check. "Such measures or means must have some relation to the end in view," explained the Indiana Supreme Court in a turn-of-the-twentieth-century case, "for, under the mere guise of the police power, personal rights and those pertaining to private property will not be permitted to be arbitrarily invaded by the legislative

—

department." If the legislature or public health authorities interfered with "the personal rights of an individual," and if they destroyed or impaired "his liberty or property," then, "under such circumstances," it became "the duty of the courts to review such legislation, and determine whether it in reality relates to, and is appropriate to secure, the object in view."[22]

As the Indiana court recognized, sometimes constitutional questions could not be avoided. When San Francisco imposed its racially targeted quarantine and inoculation orders in the spring of 1900, the Circuit Court for the Northern District of California struck it down under the Fourteenth Amendment to the U.S. Constitution. In *Wong Wai v. Williamson*, Judge William Morrow wrote that the city's orders were "boldly directed against the Asiatic or Mongolian race as a class." No evidence had been put forward to show that people of Asian descent were more liable to the plague than other people in the city. And there was not even a "pretense that previous residence, habits, exposure to disease, method of living, or physical condition has anything to do" with the discriminatory classification in question.[23] Judge Morrow ruled that such an order violated the Equal Protection Clause of the Constitution. A few weeks later, in a new case called *Jew Ho v. Williamson*, Morrow reiterated the ruling to strike down a second attempt by city authorities to accomplish the same goal of targeting the Chinese community in Chinatown.[24] Crucially, however, Morrow and the circuit court left open the very different question of whether a general quarantine and a general inoculation order would have survived review. The decisions in *Wong Wai* and *Jew Ho* did not foreclose the authority of the state to protect its population against contagion. They merely prohibited the state from doing so in a rankly discriminatory (and most likely less effective) fashion.

Even the broadest articulations of state power to fight epidemics have been accompanied by caveats and qualifications of the kind offered by Justice Harlan in *Jacobson v. Massachusetts*. Different circumstances warranted different actions, but the principles were essentially the same: courts would allow sensible public health policies to go forward, but they would retain the authority to intervene to block policies that seemed arbitrary or irrational.

—

* * *

While the courts took a middle path, public discourse around contagion remained subject to confusion and hysteria. Sometimes epidemics produced panicked overreach by the state, as in the case of the plague in San Francisco, but at other times stubborn resistance to authority rested on claims of individual liberty that have long characterized the history of epidemics in America.

Nowhere was this more evident than in the resistance to mandatory vaccination laws. In 1796, Edward Jenner in England discovered that pus in the blisters that milkmaids developed when infected with cowpox could be used to inoculate people against smallpox. Jenner's discovery soon made its way to the United States. Massachusetts became the first state to pass a law mandating smallpox vaccination, and resistance to the spread of mandatory vaccinations arose almost immediately. In 1879 William Tebb formed the Anti-Vaccination Society of America. Local organizations modeling themselves on the society soon popped up in Philadelphia, Boston, and elsewhere. Powerful opposition to vaccination arose in Milwaukee in the last quarter of the nineteenth century, culminating in anti-vaccine riots during a smallpox outbreak in the 1890s.[25] An 1894 ordinance in the city barred health authorities from isolating infectious smallpox victims without their consent. In the 1910s, anti-vaccination activists formed a powerful movement in Oregon, putting the issue up to a referendum in the state and winning a majority of the vote in Portland, though losing statewide.[26] Resistance to vaccination produced occasional libertarian victories. Utah prohibited public school officials from mandating vaccination as a condition of entrance to school in 1901.[27] Minnesota passed a similar law in 1903. California allowed those opposed to vaccination to send their children to school unvaccinated in 1911.[28] Mostly, however, objections found less formal outlets. By the early twentieth century nearly half of all states mandated vaccination for smallpox, but the penalties for noncompliance were few. (Recall that Henning Jacobson in Massachusetts was fined $5, but never compulsorily vaccinated.) Parents of school-age children willing and able to satisfy compulsory education laws

—

through private schools or home schooling could evade the requirements entirely.

The anti-vaccination movement of the nineteenth and early twentieth centuries exhibited a curious demographic mix. Older white Anglo-Saxon Protestants from rural areas resisted vaccinations because they seemed to interfere with the autonomy of traditional ways of life. Such people, living in sparsely inhabited regions, often had less reason to worry about infection anyway, which may have affected their calculations about the very modest risks posed by vaccines. Poor, urban, and immigrant communities often resisted vaccinations, too. Many residents in Polish and German immigrant communities, for example, had watched as public health officials wielding scientific expertise disrupted their urban working-class neighborhoods. The urban poor understood all too well that health officials sometimes rode roughshod over their interests.

Communities of free Blacks frequently shared some of the same suspicions. African Americans in Baltimore collectively resisted smallpox vaccination during an outbreak in 1827. Frederick Douglass voiced skepticism about vaccination: "Count me on the side of liberty," he wrote to one anti-vaccination doctor.[29] A century later Malcolm Little (later known as Malcolm X) joined the ranks of Black Americans who refused to submit to vaccinations.[30]

The poor and people of color did not limit their suspicions to vaccines. Many mid-century sanitationists believed that poverty and bad hygiene were signs of moral vice and that those who lived in dangerous slum conditions were responsible for their own predicaments.[31] New York's mid-nineteenth-century Democratic Party machine took advantage of the resulting resentments. Rallying its white ethnic immigrant base, it regularly asserted that sanitarians were biased against the poor. One Catholic newspaper with a working-class readership lampooned the board of health as the city's "In-Sanitary commission."[32] No wonder, then, that many resisted the machinery of the public health state.

Populist resentment of public health measures resurfaced in 1918 and 1919 during the flu pandemic. Authorities in San Francisco responded quickly to word of the fast-spreading illness. In October, just a few weeks

—

after the first cases had been reported, Dr. William Hassler, the chief of the city's board of health, persuaded the city supervisors to enact an ordinance requiring the wearing of masks in public places and in any place where two or more persons congregated. At first, the mask ordinance seemed to work. The San Francisco Red Cross distributed hundreds of thousands of gauze masks with strings attached to tie around the head to the city's half million residents. Use of the distinctive face coverings was widespread, and flu cases dropped dramatically. Yet as time passed, the epidemic slowed, and compliance faded. Police arrested hundreds of maskless individuals and dragged them in front of judges, who handed out fines and even a few short jail terms. Many objected that the mask order was an unconstitutional violation of their personal liberty. The city supervisors let the order lapse in mid-November, but put it back in place when cases spiked. Once again the order seemed to be successful. Yet skepticism about the efficacy of the masks, combined with the general inconvenience of the things, led to substantially less compliance with the second masking mandate than the first. Heavy-handed enforcement ensued.

Protesters responded by forming an "Anti-Mask League," insisting on their constitutional right to move about as they pleased.[33] Their claims fell within a well-established popular tradition of asserting personal freedoms over public health imperatives. Disobedience to mask laws seems not to have affected the spread of the virus too extensively. Masking rules may even have made matters worse by de-emphasizing other measures, such as social distancing, closures, and case isolation. In the end, San Francisco's death toll from the flu was not substantially different from that of other cities with less aggressive masking requirements.

* * *

Despite its persistence, the libertarian thread in American popular reaction to public health law has historically had little uptake in formal constitutional law, at either the state or federal level. Judges have been willing to give public health orders a hard second look. They have been willing to strike some orders down. But rarely have courts interfered with the basic power to keep people safe in a moment of contagion.

Considerations about what courts are good at — and what they're not — have led courts to be cautious in articulating ideas about the core values of the law in the domain of public health. Courts are ill trained to make hard judgments about the course of an infectious disease. Would the flu have killed thousands more in San Francisco without an enforceable masking requirement? Would condemnation of a tenement on Mott Street have reduced childhood deaths — or would it have produced childhood homelessness? Public health experts, not courts, have often had the best answers to these questions. Nonetheless, judges must still apply the law and keep the experts within it. American courts have historically resolved this tension by sending some difficult issues back to elected officials and back to public health experts for a second judgment. May a child gain admission to school absent a mandatory vaccination? Some courts have said yes, but almost always because the state legislature has not yet expressly said otherwise. May a resident of San Francisco challenge an order requiring quarantine and inoculation? Sometimes yes, but only because the order has been applied in a discriminatory fashion, such as by targeting the Chinese community.

When do individual rights give way to social imperatives and vice versa? Courts have usually been reluctant to say. Yet when jurists voiced ideas about values in the jurisprudence of hygiene, they typically placed social solidarity over individual liberty. Chief Justice John Marshall, as we have seen, described the police power to protect public health as a core attribute of state sovereignty.[34] Courts could and did insist that such power be exercised with rationality and competence. But otherwise, civil liberties gave way in an epidemic. That is why the U.S. Army surgeon John Billings began his 1879 essay on the "jurisprudence of hygiene" not with a proposition about individual rights, but with a claim about the duties of the state to protect "every member of the community . . . in regard to his health."[35] Such duties, said the New York Court of Appeals, gave states "the absolute control over persons and property, so far as the public health was concerned."[36] This was not the typical civil libertarian ideal; the Anti-Mask League would have protested angrily. But far from being antithetical to freedom, the public health vision of nineteenth-century jurists claimed to be freedom's realization, what Justice John Marshall Harlan dubbed "real liberty": not an "absolute right" of personal freedom, but a world of "manifold restraints" imposed "for the common good."[37]

Civil liberties in the law of public health have not been trumps. They have been guidelines by which courts have navigated enduring questions about individual rights and collective well-being.

Chapter 4

NEW SANITATIONISMS /
NEW QUARANTINISMS

In October 2014, a nurse named Kaci Hickox flew home to the United States from Sierra Leone, where she had been treating patients in the worst known outbreak of the Ebola virus.[1] Anxieties about Ebola had recently reached a fever pitch in the United States. Within the previous few weeks a New York doctor who had been treating Ebola patients in West Africa had been hospitalized and a Liberian man had died in Dallas, leaving two nurses who had cared for him ill with the disease. When Hickox landed at Newark Airport, ready to catch her connecting flight home to Maine, a hasty temperature reading incorrectly suggested she might have the infection.[2] The governors of New Jersey and New York hastily cobbled together a policy requiring a twenty-one-day quarantine for all people entering the country who had had direct contact with Ebola patients. Authorities detained Hickox in a plastic tent near the airport. Ultimately, Hickox was not held long. She challenged her New Jersey quarantine and was released into a new quarantine in Maine, which she promptly challenged again. A federal court ordered her release.[3]

Hickox was not alone. In the fall of 2014, at least forty people were quarantined in the United States out of fear that they might be infected.[4] Several hundred more were restricted to their homes by self-quarantines. Most were aid workers returning from Ebola-stricken regions.

Yet in historical perspective, perhaps the most striking feature of the Ebola panic was not the quarantines themselves, but the reaction of public health law experts. Having established vast powers for public health since the beginnings of the republic, the experts now nearly unanimously opposed quarantines and sided with Hickox and the others. In the past, public health officials had often favored the use of forceful state powers to control infection. Now they emerged as apparent civil libertarians.

—

Their reaction illustrated a new development in the law of public health in the last quarter of the twentieth century: a new synthesis of public health and civil liberties. After the mid-twentieth century, as infectious disease decreased in relative importance in the developed world, a new sanitationism emerged as perhaps the most distinctively novel feature of the law of public health. Its core idea was that civil liberties are not antagonistic to public health. To the contrary, said the new sanitarians, civil liberties are crucial to the accomplishment of the field's most important goals.

★　★　★

"It is time to close the book on infectious diseases, and declare the war against pestilence won."[5] U.S. surgeon general William H. Stewart is widely misquoted as having said this, or something like it, in 1969. Although Stewart likely made no such claim, the idea summed up the spirit of the times. Secretary of State George Marshall told the world in 1948 that humanity was at last equipped to destroy infectious disease. And in many ways the wartime and postwar decades seemed to prove him right. Alexander Fleming produced a "mould-juice" later known as penicillin just in time for its widespread use in the Second World War. Jonas Salk announced a polio vaccine on the radio in 1953. Six years later, the World Health Organization (WHO) declared a campaign to eradicate smallpox.[6] The campaign quickly produced stunning successes; the U.S. Public Health Service discontinued routine vaccination for smallpox in 1971, and nine years later, the WHO declared victory against the disease.[7] The age-old trade-off between freedoms, on the one hand, and security against contagion, on the other, seemed finally to have been left behind, thanks to the miracles of science.

The HIV/AIDS epidemic, first identified in the United States in 1981, was one of the first signs that the declaration of victory over infectious disease had been premature.[8] Within a decade of its emergence, at least 260,000 people had contracted the disease.[9] HIV, which profoundly suppresses the immune systems of infected people, is transmitted through the exchange of certain bodily fluids, notably semen and blood. Especially at risk are men who have sex with men, drug users who share needles, and recipients of infected blood transfusions. Infection can be initially asymptomatic.

The particular features of HIV/AIDS — the disease's transmission through private activities such as homosexual sex and through illicit activities such as the sharing of syringes — encouraged public health authorities to come up with alternatives to the deployment of the state powers handed down from the nineteenth-century boards of health. Activists working on behalf of those in high-risk groups insisted on new responses, too.[10] Some political leaders proposed draconian new limits on the freedom of people exposed to or suffering from the disease. But quarantines, said AIDS activists and the new sanitarians, would be counterproductive. Such measures would drive potentially infected people underground and make fighting the spread of the disease harder, not easier. The best way to combat HIV/AIDS, the new public health officials insisted, was to protect the civil liberties of the people it most affected so that they would seek testing and treatment. In the new sanitationism of the late twentieth century, public health and liberty ran together.

The new sanitarians faced resistance. Attorney General Edwin Meese openly proposed discrimination against people infected with HIV. School districts in Indiana and elsewhere excluded minors with the disease. In Florida a mob burned the family home of an infected teenager. The Reverend Jerry Falwell called AIDS "God's punishment for homosexuals" and declared the death of thousands to be a righteous judgment on homosexuality and drug use.[11] Secretary of Education William J. Bennett and Senator Jesse Helms successfully barred the federal government from producing educational materials about safe sex. In the mid-1980s, some state and local officials, including one New York judge, called for the involuntary quarantine of people infected with HIV. Others proposed using criminal law to punish those infected with the virus.

Dr. Jonathan Mann was one of the early leaders of the new sanitarian effort.[12] The charismatic Mann began his career as an epidemic intelligence officer for the Centers for Disease Control (CDC) in Atlanta in 1975. He first got into HIV/AIDS work when the CDC sent him overseas to work on the disease in Zaire. Later, at the World Health Organization in 1986, Mann founded the

—

WHO's Global Program on AIDS.[13] Mann's program reconfigured the relationship between public health and individual rights. Advocates had long seen the two as antagonists — as "two worlds that had never spoken to one another," as one public health official from the era recalled.[14] Mann, however, reimagined the two as working together. "There is a stark connection," he wrote, "between the disregard for human rights and the health and well-being of entire populations." Repressive or coercive reactions in Zaire — or in the United States, for that matter — had the effect of making the disease harder to monitor. What public health officials needed was information about and compliance with best practices like safe sex and needle hygiene. In such circumstances, Mann wrote, "respect for human rights" led to "markedly better prevention and treatment."[15]

Mann, who died tragically in a plane crash in 1998, mentored a generation of HIV/AIDS public health advocates who carried on his legacy of synthesizing rights and health. Lawrence Gostin, now a professor at Georgetown Law School, began his career in the United Kingdom, working for the rights of the mentally ill.[16] From there he

—

turned to work for the National Council for Civil Liberties in London, a long-running defender of individual rights against the state (and the organization from which the American Civil Liberties Union got its name). Returning to the United States in the late 1980s, Gostin served on the ACLU's National Board and National Executive Committee. This was hardly the résumé of a traditional public health expert. Gostin was a civil libertarian first and foremost: "I subscribed to the dominant liberal position," he later wrote, "that individual freedom is by far the preferred value to guide ethical and legal analysis."[17]

Like Mann, Gostin soon became involved in HIV/AIDS work, bringing his civil liberties background with him. "The focus on civil liberties of persons living with HIV/AIDS may seem counterintuitive," he conceded, looking back from 2004, but there were "sound reasons for avoiding coercion whenever possible."[18] Smart public health officials, he contended, had long since consigned quarantines for those infected with HIV to the dustbin of history. In an important article written in the mid-1990s, Gostin grasped the fact that in terms of public health law, even if state authority had diminished the scope of constitutional constraints like due process and equal protection of the laws, a new generation of laws against discrimination, such as the Americans with Disabilities Act, might force governments to update and improve existing and often backward public health systems. As Gostin saw it, borrowing from Mann, health was "of foundational importance" to "the exercise of rights and privileges." There was an "inextricable link," he insisted, "between health and human rights."[19]

In many respects, the new sanitarians of the late twentieth century resembled the progressive sanitarians of the middle of the nineteenth century. Gostin believed that "underlying conditions" were crucial to "physical, mental, and social well-being." Considerations such as "adequate levels of income and social status" helped determine the health of "people and populations."[20]

The new sanitarians took nineteenth-century concerns about poor living conditions and poverty and added rights and civil liberties to the mix. "Adequate protection of civil and political rights," insisted Gostin, "is not only an end in itself, but also helps ensure the effectiveness of AIDS prevention and treatment strategies." As he saw it, "civil and political rights" went "hand in hand with social and economic rights, notably the right to health."[21] Human rights advocates picked up the same point. Mary Robinson, the U.N. high commissioner for human rights, asserted that "in an environment where human rights are not fully respected, the likelihood of vulnerability to infection and further exclusion increases dramatically."[22] Indeed, as Gostin and Robinson suggested, HIV/AIDS came to be seen as "illustrative of a more general phenomenon in which individual and population vulnerability to disease" was "linked to the status of respect for human rights and dignity."[23]

Ensuring civil liberties, in other words, was now smart policy. It was the way to vindicate public health law. Officials could draw vulnerable and infected populations into prevention and treatment plans precisely by offering them the respect that civil liberties and civil rights seemed to guarantee. As the new century began, Gostin served as one of the principal drafters of a new model statute for state public health law: the Turning Point Model State Public Health Act.[24] The statute aimed to modernize and rationalize antiquated public health powers. It organized

—

public health law infrastructures and clarified the powers and duties of state and local governments. Inevitably, in its final sections it provided for criminal penalties for violating key public heath norms, though only when paired with required due process protections. Most striking, the new model statute began with a mission statement that folded civil liberties into public health in its very first sentence. The policy of the model statute is "that the health of the public be protected and promoted to the greatest extent possible through the public health system while respecting individual rights to dignity, health information privacy, nondiscrimination, due process, and other legally-protected interests." By 2007, states across the country had enacted some forty-eight bills and resolutions based on the model law.[25]

Wendy Parmet at Northeastern University also gave voice to the new sanitarian position. Parmet, who would serve as co-counsel in the first HIV / AIDS case to come before the U.S. Supreme Court, took up the civil liberties question in one of her first publications in the mid-1980s. In the old conventional view, she wrote, "AIDS is merely another facet of the age-old question of how to balance the rights of the individual against those of the community."[26] This was what Parmet called the "tragic view of public health."[27] But public health did not need to be a tragedy. Freedom and health could reinforce one another. The new sanitarians thus seemed to have solved the age-old dilemma. Trade-offs between the individual and the community were not inevitable. Criminal sanctions and quarantines, Parmet argued, were the wrong strategies for stopping the spread of disease. (Quarantine, she wrote, was "the revival of an archaic doctrine.")[28] Instead, noncoercive mechanisms would allow the modern and sophisticated public health state to accomplish its goals much more effectively. Educating high-risk groups about safe sex and condom use was one path. Making clean hypodermic needles available was another.

The new promise of such solutions made culture war efforts by Senator Helms and others all the more explosive. The Helms Amendment was a direct attack on the new mechanisms of promoting public health with rights rather than coercion. Other mechanisms favored by the new sanitarians turned toward social and eco-

—

nomic rights. Perhaps the way to fight epidemics was to find better housing for infected people so that they could get off the street and live safer and healthier lives. Or maybe the United States could restructure its health care system such that preexisting conditions would no longer be barriers to health insurance coverage. Guaranteed health insurance, such as the systems in place in much of western Europe, promised to save lives and stop the spread of disease more effectively than ham-fisted alternatives.

The new sanitarians who emerged with the HIV/AIDS crisis knew that repression produced resistance and backlash among citizens, and sought to create innovative public health law that used human desires and wishes to help control infectious disease. When Ebola arrived in the United States in 2014, the legal authorities on public health were thus already prepared to deploy the new sanitationism in defense of care providers like Kaci Hickox. HIV/AIDS had created a new paradigm. Indeed, the influence of the paradigm had been evident a decade earlier, during the SARS coronavirus outbreak in the spring of 2003. The Department of Health and

Human Services concluded that quarantine was "optimally performed on a voluntary basis," rather than a compulsory one.[29]

* * *

The new sanitarians of the late twentieth and early twenty-first centuries had a deep and lasting impact on the field of public health law. Yet real questions persisted about the future viability of the synthesis of civil liberties and public health. Protecting civil liberties traditionally meant guaranteeing private rights against state interference. The legal response to HIV/AIDS, however, revealed that the legal architecture of America's private, market-driven health care system had driven new wedges between traditional private rights and community well-being. Indeed, private health care and exclusive intellectual property rights created new forms of quarantinism to match the new sanitationism.

One dimension of the problem comes into view if we think about the institutional environments that gave rise to the great early- and mid-century triumphs over infectious disease. Neither Jonas Salk, who discovered the

—

first polio vaccine, nor Albert Sabin, who soon thereafter discovered a simpler oral polio vaccine, asserted patent rights in their discoveries. In part, this was because their research was financed by a nonprofit foundation, the National Foundation for Infantile Paralysis (later known as the March of Dimes), which had received money from the public. Nearly 80 million people had donated to the National Foundation.[30] Thousands of doctors and children had put themselves at risk to assist in the vaccine's development. To be sure, it's also true that lawyers believed patent protections might be difficult to assert because the vaccine consisted of a series of already well-known processes. But pharmaceutical firms today assert rights in methods that are less novel than the initial polio vaccines — and in methods that are worth far less. Salk and Sabin declined to assert patents that may have amounted to billions of dollars. "There is no patent," Salk famously told the journalist Edward R. Murrow with a mix of modesty and hubris. "Could you patent the sun?"[31]

Similarly, the vaccines that eradicated smallpox in the 1970s did not rely on information held as private property: smallpox vaccines had been well understood since the end of the eighteenth century. Early participants in the discovery of penicillin, the world's first antibiotic, declined to assert patent rights in their discovery, too. The absence of monopoly protections removed a possible obstacle to the antibiotic's distribution during World War II. At the same time, however, the absence of property rights in the earliest days of penicillin may have caused delays in mass production and distribution of the life-saving drug. No firm or organization stood to benefit from penicillin's success. A decade passed between the serendipitous 1928 discovery of what British scientist Alexander Fleming had at first called "mould-juice" and the beginnings of production for use in the treatment of infections.[32]

By the late twentieth century, however, the quasi-public infrastructure characterizing the great mid-century progress had given way to semi-private mechanisms of medical research, which responded to powerful financial incentives to manufacture and distribute certain medicines. Pharmaceutical firms, marshaling a vast amount of scientific and technical know-how, now took a leading role in the production of crucial life-saving medicines for infectious diseases. But privatizing urgent public health work also risked a disconnect between private property rights in scientific advancements and public health imperatives. Such rights created new monopoly power over vital new medicines. In some instances, the proliferation of patents posed obstacles to the development of new drugs.[33] Thickets of many patents held by far-flung firms — what lawyers Rebecca Eisenberg and Michael Heller called an "anti-commons" — interfered with the assembly of complex medicines.[34] In other instances, private patent rights spurred the discovery and invention of new drugs — but gave firms nearly unaccountable power to set prices, sometimes so prohibitively high as to exclude needy populations.

The new quarantinism of intellectual property rights emerged in the same HIV / AIDS context that helped produce the new sanitationism. At first, private firms were reluctant to invest in research. The returns seemed likely to be too low. In 1984, a North Carolina firm called Burroughs Wellcome, later part of the GlaxoSmithKline empire, agreed to work with the National Cancer Institute to identify potentially effective drugs for treating AIDS patients.[35] By early 1985, Burroughs Wellcome had applied for a patent on AZT, the first antiretroviral drug to show promise for treatment. Early blood tests to detect the virus were also held exclusively. And the consequences of ownership rights quickly became clear as Burroughs Wellcome set prices. A year's treatment with the AZT antiretroviral drug could cost $8,000 or more.[36] It was the most expensive drug in the country. Critics estimated that profit margins on AZT were between 40 and 80 percent and projected revenue at nearly $5 billion annually.[37]

The discovery of AZT made visible the ways in which private property mobilized the coercive force of the state to deny people life-saving treatments. In 1989, members of an organization called the AIDS Coalition to Unleash Power, or "ACT UP," dramatized the point by occupying Burroughs's offices in Research Triangle Park near Durham, North Carolina, to protest sky-high prices that excluded the poor from potentially life-saving science. ACT UP told Burroughs executives that "people who lack access are dying because they can't get your drug."[38] Law enforcement officials carried the protesters away.

Quarantinist states are typically thought to be authoritarian because they infringe on private rights such as property protections. The HIV/AIDS situation, by contrast, signaled a different mode of harmful state power. Now American law exhibited authoritarian features precisely by enforcing private firms' property rights against the needy.

It was no wonder, then, that new sanitarians like Parmet urged a reorganization of our health care system. In a world in which health care for most Americans had to be purchased on the market, and in which firms had discretion to charge whatever price the market would bear, the law of the marketplace functioned much like the cordon sanitaire of authoritarian European regimes. For centuries, crude quarantines had condemned people to grave risks of suffering and death. The new cordon sanitaire around Burroughs Wellcome's private property now had much the same effect, though it came in a new form.

Private property in medicines, in other words, was a double-edged sword. One blade slashed through obstacles to the production of new medicines by producing powerful incentives for the medical-industrial complex

---

to conduct effective research. In this sense, property in drugs reproduced the new sanitationist alignment of public health and private rights. The other blade, however, made an unkind cut. Once a new medicine had been discovered and tested, the private health care market and the property rights that sustained it enclosed scientific advances and excluded people from them. New sanitationisms, it seemed, could morph into new quarantines. Private property took on one guise ex ante — and another ex post.

* * *

As a new century dawned, another development threatened the happy congruence of civil liberties and public health. A substantial part of the new sanitationist synthesis rested on the impossibility of gathering information and controlling individuals without voluntary compliance. People facing threats of coercion, isolation, or other adverse consequences would not report reliable information about their health. People with HIV or those returning from Ebola-stricken West Africa could evade detection to avoid isolation. Quarantines could drive infections underground and deny authorities the information needed to manage risks. Civil liberties, such authorities said, were smart public health policy, far better than the hasty and crude policies of the quarantinists. And so the old draconian methods of the crude quarantine seemed futile. Accomplishing public health goals required protecting the liberties of the people affected, at least in part because, as the sanitarians saw it, there was really no other choice.

But what if the new sanitationism *wasn't* the only choice? The apparent futility of coercion in public health law was at least in part a function of a particular relationship between technology, disease, and society. Not every disease frustrates coercion as HIV does. (State laws in the last decade of the twentieth century approved new forms of coercion for drug-resistant tuberculosis, for example.)[39] In the second edition of his book *Public Health Law,* published after the terrorist attacks of 9/11, a chastened Lawrence Gostin seemed to step back from the effort to synthesize rights and health. "My devotion to civil liberties," he now wrote, "was particularly strained by events surrounding September 11."[40] Issues such as the threat of bioterrorism with infectious agents raised the prospect that individual rights and public health might once again be in tension — or even at odds.

Perhaps even more fundamentally, new technologies such as apps for cell phones and cell phone tracing threatened to alter the precarious balance between liberty and health. If states or other powerful institutions were able to develop technologies capable of testing, tracking, and tracing individuals in ways that defeated evasion, then the calculus might change. As America entered the era of the novel coronavirus in the spring of 2020, the foundations of the new sanitationist synthesis were already starting to shake.

Chapter 5

MASKED FACES TOWARD THE PAST

America's first responses to the novel coronavirus were shaped by legal and political tools inherited from the past. The imperatives of the pandemic played a role, too, of course, but history conditioned American responses.

How did history matter? Long-standing patterns in American history reemerged in the early months of the new coronavirus. As in past epidemics, the law of epidemics took the form mostly of state law, not federal. Courts retained their customary role in deferring to public health authorities — although, as usual, the courts did not cede the field entirely. There were new twists, too. This time, courts became forums for new varieties of hyper-partisanship. Novel quarantinisms appeared,

—

too, now exacerbated by mass incarceration and mass immigration detention. Glaring racial disparities in fatality rates, especially high for African Americans, reprised long-standing health injustices and produced renewed attention by progressive sanitarians to class disparities in living conditions and access to health care. Meanwhile, new technologies of surveillance threatened to undo the civil liberties synthesis of the HIV/AIDS era.

* * *

In most countries, the coronavirus crisis accelerated trends toward further concentrated power at the national instead of the local level. Sometimes, this was because presidents and prime ministers used the crisis to consolidate power. In Hungary, the parliament handed Prime Minister Viktor Orban sweeping new emergency powers. In China, President Xi Jinping used the crisis to expand his power over Hong Kong. As the legal scholar David Schleicher has observed, however, the imperatives of COVID-19 produced national centralization in countries around the world even where leaders did not use the virus as a pretext for power grabs.[1] The speed and geographical

—

scope of the crisis seemed to warrant national rather than local policy.

In the United States, by contrast, the law of public health continued to be principally state and local law. The federal government played an awkward and sometimes bumbling role.[2] The federal Centers for Disease Control and Prevention, established in Atlanta after World War II to wage an effective campaign against malaria, had developed an international reputation as a leading institution in global efforts to combat infectious diseases. Now the CDC produced flawed testing kits in the early days of the outbreak that made it impossible to test widely. CDC efforts to assist in the tracking and tracing of infected travelers proved clumsy and ineffective. (The CDC's director, Robert Redfield, had been an early and controversial proponent of quarantinist strategies for HIV/AIDS patients.) Meanwhile, the White House mostly declined to assert vigorous federal executive authority, except to advance preexisting partisan projects. Emergency orders cut back on the entry of asylum seekers and foreign workers and slashed federal funds for noncitizen students.[3] A porous travel ban slowed travel from

China while COVID-19 cases poured in from Europe. Federal officials like Anthony Fauci, the director of the National Institute of Allergy and Infectious Diseases, and Deborah Birx, the coronavirus response coordinator for the White House, became clearinghouses for information and scientific guidance. But they exercised relatively little actual authority. Instead, they issued federal standards in the form of guidance documents and best practices, not mandates carrying the force of law.

State governors filled the vacuum, relying on the public health power that the early American jurisprudence of hygiene had supplied. In New York, for example, the state legislature expanded Governor Andrew Cuomo's legal authority to deal with the epidemic.[4] Cuomo shut down nonessential businesses, banned nonessential gatherings, suspended evictions and foreclosures, and required social distancing in public venues.[5] He ordered vulnerable people such as the elderly to remain indoors except for solitary outdoor exercise. On the West Coast, Governor Gavin Newsom in California exercised broad authority, too, issuing a stay-at-home order, allocating emergency funds to protect the state's large homeless population, halting evictions, and more.[6] Governor Mike DeWine of Ohio issued a stay-at-home order prohibiting all but essential activities. Other governors, sometimes desperately and often creatively, exercised state-level legal authority over a nationwide — indeed, worldwide — crisis.

Decentralization, however, meant wide legal variation and poor coordination. States, for example, adopted different standards for what counted as an essential business. Efforts to reopen were badly mismatched.[7] Indeed, state and local divergence in coronavirus policies became a hallmark of American law's response to the new contagion.[8] Some applauded decentralization, given that different infection rates seemed to warrant different responses, depending on region. But of course nothing in a centralized response would have required a one-size-fits-all federal policy. Central decision makers routinely deliver aid to particular regions of the country. (Consider disaster relief for hurricanes, earthquakes, or fires.) And the federal government has long crafted health standards such as those regarding pollution and air quality that implicate certain regions and not others. The U.S. response was decentralized not because localism made sense under the circumstances, but because America's tenacious history of federalism channeled public health authority into state and local paths.

A century ago, public health experts expected the quarantine power to migrate from states to the federal government.[9] Infectious diseases crossed state lines without regard to jurisdictional differences; given the increasing speed of transportation and the scope of the economy, the sheer scale of infectious diseases in the modern world seemed to require such a development. But today, even if Congress tried to exercise a quarantine authority, it is not at all clear that such authority would be lawful. The federal government lacks a police power. Its authority in the area of public health arises principally out of its power to regulate interstate commerce and activities affecting interstate commerce. But in 1995, the U.S. Supreme Court ruled that the Constitution does not permit the Congress to regulate noneconomic activity that does not, on its own, substantially affect interstate commerce.[10] In 2012, in *National Federation of Independent Business (NFIB) v. Sebelius,* the Court further defined the limits on the commerce power. Five justices ruled that the Affordable Care Act requirement that individuals purchase health insurance or pay a tax went beyond Congress's commerce power.[11] The Court found a way to uphold the act's individual mandate; Chief Justice John Roberts and four other justices ruled that it could be sustained as an exercise of the federal government's taxing power.[12] But the limits on the interstate commerce authority were clear.

The decision in *NFIB v. Sebelius* threatened to rule out a federal power to enact localized quarantines within the United States.[13] Unlike a health insurance mandate, quarantine authority could not be framed as a tax. A Congress without the power to compel people to purchase health insurance may be a Congress without the power to mandate isolation and quarantines within the states.

* * *

Courts, including the U.S. Supreme Court, mostly assumed their historic role in the early months of the coronavirus pandemic, though now with a few new wrinkles. Hundreds of individuals, businesses, and organizations challenged state shutdown orders in court.[14]

In some instances, the simple threat of an adjudication led states to alter their initial social-distancing rules. For example, when the New York Civil Liberties Union charged that New York's rule prohibiting all but religious gatherings violated the First Amendment, Governor Cuomo relaxed restrictions on small groups across the board.[15] Those court challenges that actually produced a judicial determination typically lost. But some fared better.

In Wisconsin in May 2020, the state Supreme Court struck down emergency coronavirus provisions issued by Secretary Andrea Palm of the state's Department of Health Services (DHS).[16] Palm's "Order 28," issued in mid-April, was a broad assertion of public health law. The order prohibited all nonessential travel, closed down all businesses, and barred private gatherings of any number of people not in one household. Order 28 required all schools closed for the remainder of the school year and closed all places of public amusement and activity, indoors and out. It continued prior closures of hair salons and restaurants. It banned religious groups from gathering in groups of ten or more for services, including weddings and funerals. And it imposed an across-the-board six-foot social-distancing requirement for people not in a single household.

Four justices of the Wisconsin court voted to strike down Order 28 in its entirety, but they did so in a way that echoed the long history of judicial caution in the face of public health emergencies. The court declined to overrule the power of the DHS, the governor, or the state legislature to produce such regulations so long as appropriate emergency procedures were followed, but ruled that the secretary had failed to follow such procedures in promulgating Order 28.

To be sure, the Wisconsin decision was received as a highly politicized decision, pitting the state's Republican-controlled legislature, which had brought the complaint, against its Democratic-controlled executive branch. Republican partisans had protested the DHS order at the state capitol in Madison. And the four justices voting to overturn the law had been elected to the court as Republicans. (Two of them wrote separately to express withering criticism of the secretary's order.) But the novelty of the Wisconsin case was not that it was political, per se. The law of public health has always been political because disputes over the basic rights of individuals and the power of the state (in moments of public health emergency or otherwise) pose questions about the values by which we order our communities. Such disputes require resolution of basic questions. How much risk ought we to take? How valuable is human life, and what is the proper weight given to economic life and wealth? How ought we to distribute the costs of public health? Resolving such grave questions, whether in legislatures, statehouses, or courthouses, inevitably involves political judgment.

One new feature in the Wisconsin litigation and in disputes across the country was that public health law had now become deeply partisan in a way it has not usually been in our history. Undoubtedly, local controversies such as the mid-nineteenth-century dispute over the Marine Hospital on Staten Island have long had a partisan character; local Democrats there seized on public health law constraints to rally a populist base against Republican health officials. But at a state and national level, values in public health controversies rarely correlated closely with partisan affiliation. Not so in 2020. In Wisconsin, in the

—

state's Supreme Court and elsewhere, views about the law of public health in a contagion were split starkly along Republican and Democratic lines, with only one of the state's conservative justices voting with the liberal dissenters. The same partisanship was evident in an unprecedented legal development at the national level when the Republican-controlled Justice Department took the novel step of supporting a lawsuit to stop the efforts of Gretchen Whitmer, the popular Democratic governor of Michigan, to control the coronavirus. The Justice Department took no such action in other states, though many had put in place similar measures.[17]

The new partisan dimension of the law's response to the novel coronavirus was also apparent in the only coronavirus case to have made it to the U.S. Supreme Court at the time of this writing — a case that signaled an important new dimension in the law of public health even as it reaffirmed many longtime patterns. In *South Bay United Pentecostal Church v. Gavin Newsom*, plaintiffs sued the governor of California, claiming that the state's coronavirus safety requirements violated their religious freedoms. California's rules limited religious worship to 25 percent of a building's legal occupancy, or one hundred attendees, whichever was lower. The plaintiffs contended that the rule was flatly unconstitutional. A bare majority of five justices on the Supreme Court—four associate justices appointed by Democrats along with Chief Justice John Roberts—declined to intervene, leaving in place the state limits. But four justices appointed by Republican presidents dissented, arguing that the rules discriminated against religious worshippers in violation of the free exercise clause of the First Amendment.[18]

In one respect, the slender Court majority carried forward the long tradition of judicial decisions upholding state authority to fight pandemics. Churches have always been subject to the general epidemic regulations enacted under the police powers of the states. Such power goes back at least as far as the prohibitions on urban churchyard burials in the first decades of the nineteenth century.

Nonetheless, the Court's dissenters took up a religious liberty argument that in the previous several decades had become one of the central levers in conservative Republican Party critiques of the modern regulatory state. In one such challenge in 2014, *Burwell v.*

Hobby Lobby, the Supreme Court's Republican-appointed majority interpreted religious freedoms to allow corporate employers to opt out of the Affordable Care Act requirement that employer-provided health insurance include coverage for contraception.[19] In another case, *Masterpiece Cakeshop v. Colorado Civil Rights Commission,* decided in 2018, the Court ruled that a Colorado state civil rights agency's conduct in requiring that a bakery provide a cake for a same-sex couple's wedding violated the bakery owners' rights to the free exercise of their religion.[20] Two years later, in the *South Bay United Pentecostal Church* case, Justice Brett Kavanaugh's dissenting opinion did not address the state's concerns that worship involves extended social contact in ways that supermarket shopping does not. But the almost perfect partisan split in the case offered considerable evidence for a new politics in which ideas about religious liberty attacked the basic structures of the regulatory state, including the public health law powers that predate the beginnings of the republic.

A second new development in coronavirus cases in the courts arose out of the fast proliferation of so-called waivers as organizations and businesses began to reopen.

Countless businesses asked customers to waive the right to sue in the event they got sick. Even a handful of colleges and universities did the same. Efforts to use such waivers were perhaps understandable. No one knew for sure what the best practices for reopening would turn out to be; some businesses' liability insurance policies, moreover, excluded liability for pandemic-related costs, which might have left certain small businesses facing grave risks. Yet waivers also attacked a basic idea in the rule of law. They aimed to exclude the courts from the resolution of disputes.[21] By early summer 2020, there was little way to tell whether such waivers would be enforced by the courts. But several decades of increasingly broad enforcement of such agreements led many to think that waivers might have substantial effect. At the same time, state legislatures and the U.S. Congress began discussing broad legislation to immunize businesses from suits, even without a waiver.

Historian Frank Snowden writes that to study epidemics in a society "is to understand that society's structure" and "its political priorities."[22] The legal system's responses to the coronavirus controversies bear out Snowden's dictum. Decades of increased reliance on waivers by businesses of all kinds paved the way for further expansion of waiver usage during COVID reopening efforts. Decades of business-financed attacks on lawsuits smoothed the path for immunity legislation. Similarly, decades of Republican Party resistance to expertise and to the regulatory state produced a newly rambunctious partisan dissent from the basic propositions of the law of public health. In Texas, the state's governor prohibited local and city officials from enforcing rules requiring masks in public, despite wide public health consensus that mask wearing was an important tool in slowing the virus's spread. The same spirit that led to arson at the Marine Hospital on Staten Island in 1858 now produced armed partisan protest in the Michigan State House, populist resistance to mask mandates in Oklahoma, and novel religious freedom claims in the Supreme Court.

* * *

The millions of people being held in America's jails, prisons, and immigration detention centers presented one of the most impassioned COVID-19 controversies — and helped to carry forward the long tradition of authoritarian quarantines for the marginalized in American society.

The United States has the highest prison population rate in the world. At the beginning of the pandemic, nearly 1 percent of the population of the United States lived in a jail or prison or an immigration detention facility—a total of 2.1 million people.[23] No other country matched this level of incarceration. In the United Kingdom, for example, a mere eighty-one thousand people were imprisoned at the outset of the coronavirus pandemic, a rate of less than one-fourth the U.S. incarceration rate.[24] Even authoritarian China, whose population was more than four times that of the United States in 2019, imprisoned half a million fewer people.[25] Moreover, American imprisonment rates at the beginning of 2020 were not equally distributed by race.[26] Around 60 percent of prisoners were African American or Latinx even though Blacks and Latinx people made up only 30 percent of the nation's population. In many states, one in twenty adult Black men was in jail or prison.

Decades of legal decisions to facilitate mass incarceration helped create a vicious new quarantinism. In

1979, the Supreme Court upheld the short-term use of double bunking in prison cells. Two years later, the Court gave its blessing to the long-term use of double bunking. Soon, fully grown men were being held two to a cell in six-by-eight lockups.[27] Once COVID-19 entered America's crowded prisons, the results were grim. U.S. attorney general William Barr recognized in early April that at least three federal prisons were "experiencing significant levels of infection."[28] In Tennessee, seven hundred prisoners tested positive for the disease in one prison; a total of twenty-six hundred prisoners in the state had tested positive by the end of May.[29] A thousand prisoners tested positive in California by early June. Tests at the Marion Correctional Institution in Ohio found that a stunning 80 percent of the twenty-five hundred inmates had contracted the new coronavirus; at least thirteen died.[30] In effect, a substantial number of Americans were cordoned off in infectious detention. Prison walls became like the cordon sanitaire that authorities imposed on Chinese residents of San Francisco in 1900. Journalist Lawrence Wright's eerily prescient science fiction novel, *The*

End of October, published in March 2020, described a decision to shut the gates to Mecca during a pandemic, closing in millions of Muslims during the annual Hajj. That work, of course, is fiction, but American prisons did the same thing with an actual population of millions. To be sure, most of those locked in prisons with the coronavirus had been convicted of crimes, sometimes terrible ones. Some posed danger, perhaps even substantial danger, to the community. But the vastly oversized American prison system, and the use of plea bargaining as the principal mode of conviction, meant that far too many people were subjected to this new dystopian quarantine. As advocates pointed out, not one person in the prison system had been sentenced to be involuntarily exposed to a potentially deadly infectious disease.

Once upon a time, the American legal system knew how to manage prisoners in an epidemic. Colonial and nineteenth-century state law routinely dictated that vulnerable prisoners be moved to safety in times of pestilence.[31] Twenty-first-century American prison systems, by contrast, seemed to have forgotten about the risks of epidemics. They had grown complacent after a century

—

of calm. Suddenly, however, a swollen American prison system had to make thousands of extraordinary legal decisions on the continued detention of prisoners.

Many counties substantially reduced their pretrial jail populations, but such moves affected only a small percentage of those held in the criminal justice system. Connecticut released 11 percent of its sentenced prison population in the two months after the outbreak of the coronavirus, though many such releases were part of existing efforts to reduce the state's prison population.[32] In other states, prison officials did little or nothing. Pennsylvania had released a mere 150 people of its 96,000-person prison population by early May.[33] (Inmates in at least one Pennsylvania prison went on a hunger strike to protest guards not wearing required masks.)[34] By early June, observers were comparing many prison systems to the mid-twentieth-century malaria experiments financed by the U.S. Army in prisons in Illinois, Maryland, and Missouri.[35] Such experiments, which intentionally infected prisoners with the disease in hopes of finding a vaccine, proceeded for nearly thirty years until being shut down by state prison officials in 1974.[36]

—

Judges' reactions to the contagion in prisons were as wildly disparate as the responses of state prison officials. Some judges angrily rebuked prison officials and ordered the immediate compassionate release of particularly vulnerable prisoners; Judge Alison Nathan in New York condemned the Bureau of Prisons for conditioning release on what she called a "Kafkaesque" regime of successive fourteen-day group quarantines that were to be renewed each time a member of the group tested positive.[37] (Such a so-called quarantine threatened to isolate imprisoned people indefinitely until every member of the group was infected.) Other judges were substantially more deferential to prison officials. Two federal cases decided on the same day in late April raised identical challenges to prisons' refusal to release vulnerable prisoners — and produced opposite outcomes. A judge in Ohio ordered a prison to evaluate and release medically vulnerable prisoners.[38] A judge in Louisiana dismissed the prisoners' suit, declining to impose federal constitutional obligations on the prison.[39]

Two patterns emerged clearly in the prison cases. Courts declined to issue blanket release orders for inmates defined by age or offense.[40] Moreover, anecdotal evidence suggested that the legal system's individualized COVID-emergency evaluations of prisoners' fitness for release suffered from the same racist attitudes that created disproportionately minority prison populations in the first place.

★ ★ ★

COVID-19 revealed racial inequities beyond America's prison archipelago. Roughly 12 percent of the nation's population is African American but, as of early June 2020, 24 percent of the nation's COVID-19 fatalities were.[41] Accounting for the fact that Blacks are on average younger than whites, disparities in death rates were even starker: three and a half times higher among Blacks and nearly two times higher among Latinx people than among whites.[42] American Indian and Alaskan Native peoples suffered extraordinarily high rates of the disease. By late spring, five Native tribes had infection rates greater than those of any of the fifty states. The Navajo Nation in the Southwest counted nearly seven thousand cases and more than three hundred deaths.[43]

The power of state governors exacerbated conditions in some Native communities, as when Governor Kristi Noem tried to override highway health checkpoints set up by Lakota Nation peoples in South Dakota.

Much commentary about the racially unequal impact of the epidemic attributed the effects to poverty or diet or preexisting medical conditions or even (without good evidence) to genetic vulnerabilities. Other accounts flatly asserted that racism or white supremacy was the cause. With the likely exception of genetics, all of these factors concentrated the effects of the virus in already disadvantaged communities. The virus targeted the poor and disenfranchised because its spread was abetted by housing insecurity, economic inequities, crowded living conditions, poor access to health care, mass incarceration, and myriad other artifacts of disadvantage.

Less apparent, but true nonetheless, was that law shaped the divergent impacts of the coronavirus.[44] Legal rules and institutions that most people take for granted — and that usually pass as neutral and uncontroversial — laundered long histories of inequity and helped produce disparate vulnerabilities to the virus.

—

For most people living in the United States, the law of the marketplace — the basic rules of private property, contract law, and tort law — determined access to basic needs. Labor law set the terms of people's employment arrangements and established the landscape in which collective organizing happened (or did not happen). Such rules exerted powerful effects every time a custodian in Queens decided whether to take the subway ride to work in a Manhattan office building. (Studies of the coronavirus in New York quickly showed that the disease disproportionately impacted poorer outlying regions of the city where workers had little choice but to ride contaminated subway cars.) By the same token, every time immigrant workers in Nebraska considered going to their job at a meatpacking plant, the law distributing rights in the private market bore down on their decision. The foundational legal rules of the American social order determined the contours of such choices. They determined what such workers could count on if they didn't go to work, what workers would gain by going ahead, and how workers would be treated if they became ill. For some, disproportionately Black and Latinx, law produced grave risks of exposure and infection.[45] For the luckier few, disproportionately white, those same rules of private property and contract and tort offered the power to self-isolate while drawing down savings or taking advantage of other resources. The basic legal arrangements of American society compounded centuries of rank discrimination, made manifest in the disparate death rates of the coronavirus crisis.

Access to health care in the pandemic exhibited the same structure. American law at the onset of the pandemic arranged for the provision of health care through an inordinately complex set of market mechanisms made from basic legal building blocks. To be sure, the Affordable Care Act, sometimes known as "Obamacare," facilitated the availability of care for millions of Americans as the pandemic hit.[46] Still, even after Obamacare, the American law of property and tax continued to channel health insurance through employment, where it had substantial tax advantages as a form of compensation. American labor law did not require paid sick leave. But by yoking the social provision of health care to a lightly regulated private labor market, the American legal system

—

produced yet another mechanism of racial disparity. African American unemployment rates were roughly twice the unemployment rates of white Americans when the virus hit.[47] When people of color in the United States found employment, such work was disproportionately likely to be in jobs that did not offer health insurance benefits or paid sick leave. The result was that people of color were inequitably likely to suffer from poor care long before the new virus arrived, and to lack adequate access to care once it was here.

The many mechanisms of disadvantage converged in an excruciating moral dilemma that appeared as the scale of the epidemic ballooned in March 2020. If there proved not to be sufficient medical equipment to treat gravely ill virus patients, doctors began to ask what the rules would be for triaging scarce resources. The most prominent example was the ventilator, a device that delivers oxygen to the lungs of patients unable to breathe on their own. What if there were more patients in need of ventilators than there were ventilators available?

The usual answers to such questions had been worked out over years by medical ethicists and moral philosophers. Standard resolutions considered the age of the patient, the health conditions of the patient, and their expected life years remaining. Maximizing "QALYs" — quality-adjusted life years — was the state-of-the-art answer. Immediately, however, advocates for the aged and disabled objected because this approach openly disadvantaged them. Furthermore, the life expectancy of white Americans was nearly four years longer than that of Black Americans.[48] The average life expectancy of Americans in the top income quartile exceeded that of Americans in the bottom income quartile by ten years.[49] Implicitly, therefore, the QALY method of running a triage system further disadvantaged the already disadvantaged, whose poverty or poor medical care had reduced their life expectancy. Triaging systems reproduced and reflected discriminations that had helped cause disparate health and life expectancies in the first place.

A decent society that relies in ordinary times on private property and the market to create and distribute wealth and flourishing must have legal arrangements that are up to the task of providing for basic needs in crisis times. Therein lies the wisdom in the ancient Cice-

—

ronian idea that the health of the people is the supreme law. American legal rules and institutions utterly failed to enact this moral imperative in the coronavirus emergency.

★ ★ ★

The coronavirus also occasioned a new wave of ugly criminal violence against people of Asian descent.[50] From early in the outbreak, the pandemic's apparent origins in the city of Wuhan, China, led to assaults and harassment of people perceived as Chinese. Asian Americans reported being spat on and physically attacked in public parks, on public transportation, and in supermarkets and stores. People of Asian appearance reported having objects thrown at them from passing cars and being sprayed with disinfectant. Although epidemiologists conclusively linked the genetic structure of most coronavirus cases in the United States to European strains of the virus, Asian-owned stores were vandalized with graffiti about the so-called China virus. One mother reported that a white man knocked her seven-year-old Asian American daughter from her bike and yelled that she should leave the country because she was infecting others.

—

The anti-Asian assaults of 2020 reprised 175 years of suspicions about the contagiousness of Asian immigrants. From Chinese exclusion in the late nineteenth century to the medical inspections at Angel Island to the bubonic plague quarantines of 1900, America has long been fertile for another outbreak of racially motivated crime. And as the pandemic grew worse, the White House got into the business of creating new rules aimed at Chinese residents. In May, President Trump moved to ban certain groups of Chinese graduate students and researchers. His aides defended the ban as a countermeasure against industrial espionage. But the timing suggested that the president was adding his weight to the thuggish attackers who had been spitting on and attacking people of Asian descent for months.

* * *

By early summer 2020, a further quarantinist risk loomed on the horizon. The United States often prefers to present itself in liberal terms. But our mixed track record makes us vulnerable to dangerous paths. And few dimensions of the coronavirus crisis have been as fraught with

—

danger as the prospect of new technologies that would allow the government to track and trace people's movements and contacts.

For nearly half a century before the coronavirus pandemic, American experts in the law of epidemics had been moving toward a synthesis of civil liberties and public health. Voluntary compliance replaced coercive mandates as the favored strategy for combating infection. The cell phone and other technologies may change all that.[51] Observers around the world praised South Korean authorities for successfully slowing the spread of the virus in early 2020. But the success of the South Korean Ministry of the Interior rested on a mandate that allowed officials to track and trace the movement of all people in the country.[52] The ministry developed a contact-tracing app for cell phones and required all citizens to install it so that their movements could be monitored. If people became infected, officials could use the app to reconstruct their past contacts. South Korean public health authorities also used the app to track people in real time, monitoring whether people violated the stringent Korean quarantine rules.

Chinese officials went even further, using drones, facial-recognition cameras, and Quick Response (or QR) code technologies to monitor and track people within the country's borders.[53]

Of course, technology in itself need not pose civil liberties threats. The whole point of the synthesis of civil liberties and public health is that voluntary compliance often works better than government mandates; in theory, technology could facilitate the happy convergence of rights and welfare. But early experience with new technology in the era of the new coronavirus suggested that liberty and health might be splitting apart. In Singapore, state authorities developed a sophisticated app called TraceTogether, which allowed Ministry of Health officials to access data on users' cell phones.[54] At first, installation of the app was voluntary. The results were dismal. Less than a quarter of phone users in Singapore installed it, badly reducing the app's effectiveness and leading the government to warn that it might require installation of the app in areas experiencing severe outbreaks.[55] Australian officials experienced similar difficulties. Their voluntary COVIDSafe app induced only about half of the desired installations.[56]

Different technologies pose different levels of threat. A white paper by the American Civil Liberties Union in the midst of the spring 2020 panic set out civil libertarian standards for tracing and tracking technologies.[57] The ACLU urged that all such tech be, among other things, voluntary, nonpunitive, and nondiscriminatory. In particular, civil libertarians advocated the adoption of Bluetooth technologies that would allow public health authorities to reconstruct the proximity of a sick person's phone with other phones, as opposed to GPS technologies that would allow such authorities to pinpoint a user's physical location.

Either way, the new tech and contact-tracing mechanisms suggested that the convergence of civil liberties and public health may in fact have been a temporary synthesis, occasioned by limits in tracking and surveillance technology and by the etiology of particular diseases such as HIV / AIDS. In the era of COVID-19, a new vision of quarantinism loomed.

Afterword

VIRAL PROTESTS

Nationwide protests in late May and June 2020 arose just as the United States tried to reopen after two months of widespread COVID-19 shutdowns. The death of an African American man named George Floyd at the hands of Minneapolis police produced an outpouring of dissent and anger like none seen since at least the mass protests of 1968.

Protesters aimed to bring an end to some of the same inequities the law of epidemics had made visible over the past several centuries. From the earliest seventeenth-century settler-colonial quarantines to the yellow fever policies of the late eighteenth and nineteenth centuries to the border inspections in Texas and California

—

to the virus of the spring of 2020 and beyond, American legal responses to epidemics have targeted the poor, people at the border, and nonwhites. America's record on infectious disease is filled with discriminations and authoritarianisms. Each new infection presents a risk of entrenching existing inequities.

On the other hand, epidemics have repeatedly offered a vantage from which to see deep into basic structures of inequality and injustice in the American legal order. As the nineteenth-century jurisprudence of hygiene made apparent, calamity can be an occasion for making intolerable social conditions visible — and for reforming them. Progressive sanitarians turned contagion risks into opportunities for lifting up the poor. Savvy political leaders grasped the ways in which public health could sometimes align the interests of rich and poor, white and Black, citizen and immigrant. Disease specialists found ways to connect civil liberties and collective welfare.

—

America has two histories: one ugly, the other far more appealing. In the months and years ahead, Americans will hold the power to choose between them. Let's make the right choice.

NOTES

INTRODUCTION

1. Karl Marx, "The Eighteenth Brumaire of Louis Napoleon," in Karl Marx and Friedrich Engels, *Collected Works* 103 (1979).

2. Ernst Freund, *The Police Power: Public Policy and Constitutional Rights* 3 (1904).

3. Bryan Garner, ed., *Black's Law Dictionary,* 11th ed. (2019).

4. *Hamilton v. Kentucky Distilleries & Warehouse Co.*, 251 U.S. 146, 156 (1919).

5. Richard A. Primus, "The Limits of Enumeration," 124 *Yale Law Journal* 576 (2014).

6. Peter Baldwin, *Contagion and the State in Europe, 1830–1930* (2009).

7. Alfred Crosby, "Virgin Soil Epidemics as a Factor in the Aboriginal Depopulation in America," 33 *William & Mary Quarterly* 289, 293 (1976); Russell Thornton, *American Indian Holocaust and Survival* 22–25 (1987).

8. Edwin H. Ackerknecht, "Anticontagionism between 1821 and 1867," 22 *Bulletin of the History of Medicine* 562 (1948).

—

CHAPTER 1. THE SANITATIONIST STATE

1. Elizabeth A. Fenn, *Pox Americana: The Great Smallpox Epidemic of 1775–82* (2001).

2. Jim Downs, *Sick from Freedom: African-American Illness and Suffering during the Civil War and Reconstruction* (2012).

3. David Patterson. "Yellow Fever Epidemics and Mortality in the United States, 1693–1905," 34 *Social Science & Medicine* 855 (1992).

4. Kathryn Olivarius, "Immunity, Capital, and Power in Antebellum New Orleans," 124 *American Historical Review* 425 (2019).

5. Charles E. Rosenberg, *The Cholera Years: The United States in 1832, 1849, and 1866* (1962).

6. John Locke, "Fundamental Constitutions of Carolina (1669)," in *John Locke: Political Essays,* edited by Mark Goldie 160–61 (1997).

7. For example, *Laws of the Commonwealth of Pennsylvania, from the Fourteenth Day of October, One Thousand Seven Hundred,* 5:274 (1812).

8. *Acts and Laws of His Majesty's English Colony of Connecticut* 225 (1750).

9. "An Act to Prevent the Bringing in and Spreading of Infectious Distempers in This State, Passed 4th May, 1784," in *Laws and Ordinances Ordained and Established by the Mayor, Aldermen and Commonalty of the City of New-York, in Common Council Convened* 76 (1793).

10. "An Act to Provide against Infectious and Pestilential Diseases (1801)," in *Laws of the State of New York* 1:367 (1802).

11. An Act for Establishing an Health-Office, 1793 Pa. Laws 553.

12. George Washington, *The Ordinances of the City of Philadelphia. To Which Are Prefixed, the Act of Incorporation, and the Several Supplements Thereto* 21 (1798).

13. An Act, to Amend an Act, Instituted, an Act Reducing into One the Several Acts to Oblige Vessels Coming from Foreign Parts to Perform Quarantine, 1803 Va. Acts 350.

—

14. On the Imprisonment of Persons Arrested on Civil Process, 1836 Miss. Laws 1082.

15. Of the Preservation of the Public Health, Quarantine, Nuisance, and Offensive Trades, 1837 Mich. Pub. Acts 163.

16. Louise Carroll Wade, *Chicago's Pride: The Stockyards, Packingtown, and Environs in the Nineteenth Century* 140–41 (1987).

17. Lemuel Shattuck et al., *Report of the Sanitary Commission of Massachusetts 1850* (1948).

18. George Rosen et al., "The Metropolitan Board of Health – One Hundred Years Later," 56 *American Journal of Public Health* 699 (1966).

19. *Laws of the State of New York relating to the Metropolitan Board of Health and to the Metropolitan Board of Excise, Passed in 1866 & 1867* 18 (1867).

20. Hendrik Hartog, "Pigs and Positivism," 1985 *Wisconsin Law Review* 899, 922–24 (1985); also Hendrik Hartog, *Public Property and Private Power: The Corporation of the City of New York in American Law, 1730–1870* 150–51 (1983).

21. For example, *Gow v. Gans S.S. Line,* 174 F. 215 (2d Cir. 1909).

22. *Dubois v. City Council of Augusta,* 1 Dudley 30 (Ga. 1831); also William J. Novak, *The People's Welfare: Law and Regulation in Nineteenth-Century America* 209 (1996).

23. *Stiles v. Jones,* 3 Yeates 491 (Pa. 1803).

24. *State v. Smith,* 10 N.C. 378, 380 (1824).

25. *Gibbons v. Ogden,* 22 U.S. 1, 79 (1824).

26. *Commonwealth v. Alger,* 61 Mass. 53, 86 (1851) (Shaw, C.J.).

27. *Milne v. Davidson,* 5 Mart. (n.s.) 409, 414 (1827).

28. *Ferguson v. City of Selma,* 43 Ala. 398, 399 (1869).

29. *Brick Presbyterian Church v. Mayor of New York,* 5 Cow 538 (N.Y. Sup. Ct. 1826).

30. Novak, *The People's Welfare.*

31. *Coates v. Mayor of New York,* 7 Cow 585 (N.Y. Sup. Ct. 1827).

32. *Van Wormer v. Mayor of Albany,* 15 Wend. 262 (N.Y. 1836).

33. *Metropolitan Board of Health v. Heister,* 37 N.Y. 661, 670 (1868).

34. John S. Billings, "Jurisprudence of Hygiene," in *A Treatise on Hygiene and Public Health* 34 (1879).

35. George Edward Male, *An Epitome of Juridical or Forensic Medicine for the Use of Medical Men, Coroners, and Barristers* (1816; repr., 1819).

36. Stephen West Williams, *A Catechism of Medical Jurisprudence* (1835).

37. Samuel Farr, *Elements of Medical Jurisprudence* (1819).

38. Farr, *Elements of Medical Jurisprudence* 78.

39. Shattuck et al., *Report of the Sanitary Commission of Massachusetts 1850.*

40. Billings, "Jurisprudence of Hygiene," 34.

41. Peter Baldwin, *Contagion and the State in Europe, 1830–1930* 26 (2009).

42. John H. Griscom, *The Sanitary Condition of the Laboring Population of New York* (1845).

43. John Duffy, *The Sanitarians* 178 (1990).

44. Duffy, *Sanitarians,* 208.

45. Marjorie N. Field, *Lillian Wald: A Biography* (2009).

46. Nancy Tomes, *The Gospel of Germs* 267 (1998).

47. Florence Kelley, *Some Ethical Gains through Legislation* 230 (1905); Kathryn Kish Sklar, *Florence Kelley and the Nation's Work* 266 (1995); Felice Batlan, "Notes from the Margins: Florence Kelley and the Making of Sociological Jurisprudence," in Daniel W. Hamilton et al., eds., *Transformations in American Legal History: Essays in Honor of Professor Morton J. Horwitz* 239 (2010).

48. Upton Sinclair, *Damaged Goods* 158 (1913).

49. Edwin Chadwick, *Report on the Sanitary Condition of the Labouring Population of Great Britain* (1842).

—

50. Samuel E. Finer, *The Life and Times of Sir Edwin Chadwick* 187 (1952).

51. Chadwick, *Report on the Sanitary Condition.*

52. Jill Elaine Hasday, *Family Law Reimagined* 125–26 (2014).

53. Naomi Rogers, *Dirt and Disease: Polio Before FDR* 50 (1992).

54. Robert H. Wiebe, *The Search for Order, 1877–1920* (1967) (describing American "island communities" of the nineteenth century).

CHAPTER 2. QUARANTINISM IN AMERICA

1. Rana A. Hogarth, *Medicalizing Blackness: Making Racial Difference in the Atlantic World, 1780–1840* 30–33 (2017); Mathew Carey, *A Short Account of the Malignant Fever, Lately Prevalent in Philadelphia: With a Statement of the Proceedings That Took Place on the Subject in Different Parts of the United States* (1793).

2. Absalom Jones and Richard Allen, *A Narrative of the Proceedings of the Black People, during the Late Awful Calamity in Philadelphia, in the Year 1793: And a Refutation of Some Censures, Thrown upon Them in Some Late Publications* (1794).

3. Elizabeth C. Tandy, "Quarantine and Inoculation for Smallpox in the American Colonies (1620–1775)," 13 *American Journal of Public Health* 203, 204 (1923).

4. Elizabeth A. Fenn, "Biological Warfare in Eighteenth-Century North America: Beyond Jeffery Amherst," 86 *Journal of American History* 1552 (2000).

5. Kathryn Olivarius, "Immunity, Capital, and Power in Antebellum New Orleans," 124 *American Historical Review* 425 (2019).

6. "An Act for Establishing a Health Office, and to Secure the City and Port of Philadelphia from the Introduction of Pestilential and Contagious Diseases, and for Other Purposes," *Laws of the Commonwealth of Pennsylvania* ch. 4483, 5 (1818).

7. Jim Downs, *Sick from Freedom: African-American Illness and Suffering during the Civil War and Reconstruction* (2012).

8. Tera Hunter, *To 'Joy My Freedom: Southern Black Women's Lives and Labors after the Civil War* 24 (1997).

9. William J. Novak, *The People's Welfare: Law and Regulation in Nineteenth-Century America* 215 (1996).

10. Felice Batlan, "Law in the Time of Cholera: Disease, State Power, and Quarantines Past and Future," 80 *Temple Law Review* 53, 94 (2007).

11. Judith W. Leavitt, *Typhoid Mary: Captive to the Public's Health* 70–95 (1996).

12. Nayan Shah, *Contagious Divides: Epidemics and Race in San Francisco's Chinatown* 120–56 (2001).

13. William F. Deverell, *Whitewashed Adobe* 182–91 (2004).

14. Hunter, *'Joy My Freedom* 204.

15. Susan Reverby, *Examining Tuskegee: The Infamous Syphilis Study and Its Legacy* 67 (2009).

16. Frank M. Snowden, *Epidemics and Society: From the Black Death to the Present* 437–39 (2019).

17. 133 *Congressional Record* 38057 (1987).

18. CDC, "HIV and AIDS, United States, 1981–2000," *CDC Morbidity and Mortality Weekly Report* (2001).

19. Hidetaka Hirota, *Expelling the Poor: Atlantic Seaboard States and the Nineteenth-Century Origins of American Immigration Policy* (2017); Gerald L. Neuman, *Strangers to the Constitution* (2000).

20. Hirota, *Expelling the Poor*.

21. Neuman, *Strangers*.

22. Gerald L. Neuman, "The Lost Century of Immigration Law (1776–1885)," 93 *Columbia Law Review* 1833 (1993).

23. Joan Trauner, "The Chinese as Medical Scapegoats in San Francisco, 1870–1905," 57 *California History* 70 (1978).

24. Kathryn Stephenson, "The Quarantine War: The Burning of

—

the New York Marine Hospital in 1858," 119 *Public Health Reports* 79 (2004).

25. Lucy E. Salyer, *Laws as Harsh as Tigers* 59–61 (1995); Robert Barde and Gustavo J. Bobonis, "Detention at Angel Island: First Empirical Evidence," 30 *Social Science History* 103 (2006).

26. Patrick Ettinger, "Angel Island: United States Immigration Station, Angel Island Detention Barracks, Angel Island, Calif.," 97 *Journal of American History* 135 (2010).

27. Act of May 27, 1796, ch. 31, 1 Stat. 474.

28. Act of February 25, 1799, ch. 12, 1 Stat. 619.

29. Michael Les Benedict, "Contagion and the Constitution: Quarantine Agitation from 1859 to 1866," 12 *Journal of the History of Medicine* 177 (April 1970).

30. Act of February 15, 1893, ch. 114, § 9, 27 Stat. 449.

31. See, for example, *Congressional Record* 2177–2183 (March 22, 1882) (comments of Rep. Thomas Browne [R-IN06]).

32. 26 Stat. 1084, c. 551 (March 3, 1891).

33. Daniel Okrent, *The Guarded Gate* 284, 324 (2019).

34. Kitty Calavita, *Inside the State: The Bracero Program, Immigration, and the INS* (1992).

35. John Mckiernan-González, *Fevered Measures: Public Health and Race at the Texas-Mexico Border, 1848–1942* 5, 247 (2012).

36. Alexandra Minna Stern, "Buildings, Boundaries, and Blood: Medicalization and Nation-Building on the U.S.-Mexico Border, 1910–1930," 79 *Hispanic American Historical Review* 41 (1999).

37. Nancy Stepan, "The Interplay between Socio-economic Factors and Medical Science: Yellow Fever Research, Cuba and the United States," 8 *Social Studies of Science* 397–423 (1978).

38. Marixa Lasso, *Erased: The Untold Story of the Panama Canal* 107–33 (2019); Alexandra Minna Stern, "The Public Health Service in the Panama Canal: A Forgotten Chapter of U.S. Public Health," 120 *Public Health Reports* 675, 678 (2005).

39. *DuBois v. Augusta,* 1 Dudley 30 (Ga. 1831).

40. *Mayor, Aldermen & Commonalty of City of New York v. Miln,* 36 U.S. 102, 161 (1837).

41. Tony Allan Freyer, *The Passenger Cases and the Commerce Clause* (2014).

42. *Smith v. Turner,* 48 U.S. 283, 400 (1849).

43. *Henderson v. Mayor of City of New York,* 92 U.S. 259 (1875).

44. Sarah H. Cleveland, "Powers Inherent in Sovereignty: Indians, Aliens, Territories, and the Nineteenth-Century Origins of Plenary Power over Foreign Affairs," 81 *Texas Law Review* 1 (2002).

45. *Chae Chan Ping v. United States,* 130 U.S. 581, 608 (1889).

46. *Jacobson v. Commonwealth of Massachusetts,* 197 U.S. 11, 25 (1905).

47. Michael Willrich, *Pox: An American History* 334 (2011).

48. *Buck v. Bell,* 274 U.S. 200, 207 (1927).

49. *Jacobson,* 197 U.S. at 38; Wendy E. Parmet, "Rediscovering *Jacobson* in the Era of COVID-19," 100 *Boston University Law Review* (forthcoming July 2020).

CHAPTER 3. CIVIL LIBERTIES IN AN EPIDEMIC?

1. Jesse Leavenworth, "Rhode Island National Guard Sets Up Checkpoints," *Hartford Courant,* April 2, 2020.

2. Andrew Solender, "Coronavirus Has Boosted Unpopular Governors," *Forbes,* May 7, 2020.

3. Eli Sherman and Ted Nesi, "Cuomo Threatens to Sue Raimondo," *WPRI* [Providence, R.I.], March 28, 2020.

4. "ACLU of Rhode Island Responds," March 29, 2020, at https://www.aclu.org/press-releases/aclu-rhode-island-responds-governors-latest-order-against-out-state-drivers.

5. Katherine Gregg, "R.I. Conservative Group . . . May Sue over Coronavirus Shutdown," *Providence Journal,* May 13, 2020.

6. Gregg, "R.I. Conservative Group."

7. Rossiter Johnson and John Howard Brown, *The Twentieth Century Biographical Dictionary of Notable Americans* 360 (1904); Second Circuit Historical Committee, *The United States Attorney for the Southern District of New York: The First 100 Years (1789–1889)* 80–81, 88–89 (1987).

8. George Bliss Jr., "Office of the Attorney, Metropolitan Board of Health, November 20, 1866," in *Annual Report of the Metropolitan Board of Health* 675 (1866).

9. Bliss, "Office of the Attorney" 678.

10. George Bliss Jr., "Office of Council, Metropolitan Board of Health, December 24, 1867," in *Annual Report of the Metropolitan Board of Health* 443 (1867).

11. *People v. Roff*, 3 Park. Crim. 216, 233 (N.Y. 1856).

12. *Commissioners of Salisbury v. Powe*, 51 N.S. (6 Jones) 134, 136–37 (1858).

13. *Markham v. Brown*, 37 Ga. 277 (1867).

14. *Pinkham v. Dorothy*, 55 Me. 135 (1867).

15. *Sumner v. Philadelphia*, 6 Am. Law T. Rep. 476 (C.C.E.D. Pa. 1873).

16. *Health Department of City of New York v. Dassori*, 47 N.Y.S. 641 (App. Div., 1st Dept. 1897), app. dismissed by *Health Department of City of New York v. Dassori*, 159 N.Y. 245 (1899).

17. *Health Dept of City of New York v. Knoll*, 70 N.Y. 530 (1877).

18. *State v. Burdge*, 70 N.W. 347 (Wis. 1897).

19. *Potts v. Breen*, 167 Ill. 67 (1897); *Mathews v. Kalamazoo Board of Education*, 86 N.W. 1036, 1037 (Mich. 1901); *Osborn v. Russell*, 64 Kans. 507 (1902).

20. *State ex rel. Freeman v. Zimmerman*, 86 Minn. 353, 356 (1902).

21. *Mathews*, 86 N.W. at 1037.

22. *Blue v. Beach*, 56 N.E. 89, 93 (Ind. 1900).

23. *Wong Wai v. Williamson*, 103 F. 1 (C.C.N.D. Calif. 1900).

—

24. *Jew Ho v. Williamson,* 103 F. 10 (1900).

25. Judith Walzer Leavitt, *The Healthiest City* (1982; repr., 1996).

26. Robert D. Johnston, *The Radical Middle Class* (2003).

27. Michael Willrich, *Pox: An American History* 278–80 (2011).

28. *Williams v. Wheeler,* 138 Pac. Rep. 937 (1913).

29. Frederick Douglass to Professor J. Dobson, December 25, 1882, in *Testimonies concerning Vaccination and Its Enforcement* 31 (1892).

30. Malcolm X, *The Autobiography of Malcolm X, as Told to Alex Haley* 193 (1964; repr., 1992); Robert D. Johnston, *The Radical Middle Class* 182 (2003).

31. John Duffy, *The Sanitarians* 99 (1990).

32. Charles E. Rosenberg, *The Cholera Years: The United States in 1832, 1849, and 1866* 208 (1962).

33. Alfred W. Crosby, *America's Forgotten Pandemic* 105 (1989).

34. *Gibbons v. Ogden,* 22 U.S. 1, 203 (1824).

35. John Billings, "Jurisprudence of Hygiene," in *A. H. Buck's Treatise on Public Health* (1879), quoted in William J. Novak, *The People's Welfare: Law and Regulation in Nineteenth-Century America* 195 (1996).

36. *Metropolitan Board of Health v. Heister,* 37 N.Y. 661, 670 (1868).

37. *Jacobson,* 197 U.S. at 26.

CHAPTER 4. NEW SANITATIONISMS / NEW QUARANTINISMS

1. American Civil Liberties Union and Yale Global Health Justice Partnership, "Fear, Politics, and Ebola: How Quarantines Hurt the Fight against Ebola and Violate the Constitution" (2015), https://www.aclu.org/sites/default/files/field_document/aclu-ebolareport.pdf.

2. Kaci Hickox, "Caught between Civil Liberties and Public Safety Fears: Personal Reflections from a Healthcare Provider Treating Ebola," 11 *Journal of Health & Biomedical Law* 9, 13 (2015).

—

3. Robert Gatter, "Quarantine Controversy: Kaci Hickox v. Governor Chris Christie," 43 *Hastings Center Report* 7 (2016).

4. Jolie Kaner and Sarah Schaack, "Understanding Ebola: The 2014 Epidemic," 12 *Globalization and Health* 53 (2016).

5. Brad Spellberg and Bonnie Taylor-Blake, "On the Exoneration of Dr. William H. Stewart: Debunking an Urban Legend," 2 *Infectious Diseases of Poverty* 3 (2013).

6. Centers for Disease Control and Prevention, "History of Smallpox," August 30, 2016, https://www.cdc.gov/smallpox/history/history.html.

7. Centers for Disease Control and Prevention, "Vaccinia (Smallpox) Vaccine Recommendations of the Immunization Practices Advisory Committee (ACIP)," 40 *CDC Morbidity and Mortality Weekly Report* 1 (1991); Frank M. Snowden, *Epidemics and Society: From the Black Death to the Present* 109 (2019).

8. Aran Ron and David E. Rogers, "AIDS in the United States: Patient Care and Politics," 118 *Daedalus* 41 (1989).

9. J. Chin, "Global Estimates of HIV Infections and AIDS Cases: 1991," 5 *AIDS* 2:S57-61 (1991); James W. Curran and Harold W. Jaffe, "AIDS: The Early Years and CDC's Response," 60 *CDC Morbidity and Mortality Weekly Report* 4 (2011).

10. Steven Epstein, *Impure Science: AIDS Activism and the Politics of Knowledge* (1998).

11. Hans Johnson and William Eskridge, "The Legacy of Falwell's Bully Pulpit," *Washington Post*, May 19, 2007.

12. Lawrence O. Gostin, "A Tribute to Jonathan Mann: Health and Human Rights in the AIDS Pandemic," 26 *Journal of Law, Medicine & Ethics* 256 (1998).

13. Philip J. Hilts, "Jonathan Mann, AIDS Pioneer, Is Dead at 51," *New York Times*, September 4, 1998.

14. Hilts, "Jonathan Mann."

15. Jonathan Mann et al., eds., *Health and Human Rights: A Reader* (1999).

16. Geoff Watts, "Lawrence Gostin: Legal Activist in the Cause of Global Health," 386 *Lancet* 2133 (2015).

17. Lawrence O. Gostin, *Public Health Law: Power, Duty, Restraint* xxv (2008).

18. Lawrence O. Gostin, *AIDS Pandemic: Complacency, Injustice, and Unfulfilled Expectations* 43 (2004).

19. Lawrence O. Gostin, "Securing Health or Just Health Care? The Effect of the Health Care System on the Health of America," 39 *Saint Louis University Law Journal* 7, 10 (1994).

20. Gostin, *AIDS Pandemic* 12.

21. Gostin, *AIDS Pandemic* 81.

22. Gostin, *AIDS Pandemic* 64.

23. Gostin, *AIDS Pandemic* 67.

24. Turning Point Public Health Statute Modernization Collaborative, "Turning Point Model State Public Health Act: A Tool for Assessing Public Health Laws," September 16, 2003, http://www.publichealthlaw .net/ModelLaws/index.php.

25. Center for Law and the Public's Health, "The Turning Point Model State Public Health Act State Legislative Update Table," August 15, 2007, http://www.publichealthlaw.net/Resources/ResourcesPDFs /MSPHA%20LegisTrack.pdf.

26. Wendy Parmet, "Book Review," 12 *American Journal of Law & Medicine* 503 (1986).

27. Wendy Parmet, "Book Review: *Public Health Law: Power, Duty, Restraint,* by Lawrence O. Gostin," 24 *Journal of Public Health Policy* 460, 465 (2003).

28. Wendy Parmet, "AIDS and Quarantine: The Revival of an Archaic Doctrine," 14 *Hofstra Law Review* 53, 83 (1985).

29. U.S. Department of Health and Human Services, *HHS Pandemic Influenza Plan* S8-6, S8-9 (2005), https://www.cdc.gov/flu/pdf

/professionals/hhspandemicinfluenzaplan.pdf; also Nan D. Hunter, *The Law of Emergencies: Public Health and Disaster Management* 160 (2009).

30. Brian Palmer, "Jonas Salk: Good at Virology, Bad at Economics," *Slate*, April 13, 2014.

31. Jane E. Smith, *Patenting the Sun: Polio and the Salk Vaccine* 338 (1990).

32. Eric Lax, *The Mold in Dr. Florey's Coat: The Story of the Penicillin Miracle* 162–76 (2004).

33. Amy Kapczynski et al., "Addressing Global Health Inequities: An Open Licensing Approach for University Innovations," 20 *Berkeley Technology Law Journal* 1031 (2005).

34. Rebecca Eisenberg and Michael Heller, "Can Patents Deter Innovation? The Anticommons in Biomedical Research," 280 *Science* 698, 698–701 (1998).

35. David France, *How to Survive a Plague: The Inside Story of How Citizens and Science Tamed AIDS* 175 (2016).

36. France, *How to Survive a Plague* 297.

37. France, *How to Survive a Plague* 375.

38. France, *How to Survive a Plague* 341.

39. Lawrence O. Gostin, Scott Burris, and Zita Lazzarini, "The Law and the Public's Health: A Study of Infectious Disease Law in the United States," 99 *Columbia Law Review* 59 (1999).

40. Elizabeth Weeks Leonard, "Book Review: Lawrence O. Gostin, *Public Health Law: Power, Duty, Restraint*," 9 *Houston Journal of Health Law & Policy* 181, 188 (2009); also Parmet, "Book Review: *Public Health Law*" 465.

CHAPTER 5. MASKED FACES TOWARD THE PAST

1. David Schleicher (@ProfSchleich), Twitter, March 27, 2020, https://twitter.com/ProfSchleich/status/1243535584796295168.

2. Polly Price, "A Coronavirus Quarantine in America Could Be a Giant Legal Mess," *Atlantic*, February 16, 2020.

—

3. Zolan Kanno-Youngs and Maggie Haberman, "Trump Administration Moves to Solidify Restrictive Immigration Policies," *New York Times*, June 12, 2020.

4. Jimmy Vielkind, "New Law Expands Cuomo's Power during Coronavirus Outbreak," *Wall Street Journal*, March 3, 2020.

5. N.Y. Executive Order No. 202 (March 7, 2020).

6. Calif. Executive Order N-33-20 (March 4, 2020); Calif. Executive Order N-32-20 (March 18, 2020); Calif. Executive Order N-28-20 (March 16, 2020).

7. Rick Rojas, "Trump Criticizes Georgia Governor for Decision to Reopen State," *New York Times*, April 22, 2020.

8. Polly Price, "Do State Lines Make Public Health Emergencies Worse? Federal versus State Control of Quarantine," 67 *Emory Law Journal* 491 (2017); also Polly Price, "Sovereignty, Citizenship, and Public Health in the United States," 17 *N.Y.U. Journal of Legislation & Public Policy* 919 (2014).

9. Edwin Maxey, "Federal Quarantine Laws," 43 *American Law Review* 382, 382 (1909).

10. *United States v. Lopez*, 514 U.S. 549 (1995).

11. *National Federation of Independent Business (NFIB) v. Sebelius*, 567 U.S. 519 (2012).

12. John Fabian Witt, "The Secret History of the Chief Justice's Obamacare Decision," in Nathaniel Persily, Gillian Metzger, and Trevor Morrison, eds., *The Health Care Case: The Supreme Court's Decision and Its Implications* 215–24 (2013).

13. Arjun K. Jaikumar, "Red Flags in Federal Quarantine: The Questionable Constitutionality of Federal Quarantine after *NFIB v. Sebelius*," 114 *Columbia Law Review* 677 (2014).

14. The law firm Hunton Andrews Kurth dealt with nearly 260 lawsuits challenging business closure orders by late June 2020. In all, the Hunton firm counted more than 3,000 lawsuits arising out of COVID-19 by the end of June. See https://www.huntonak.com/en/covid-19-tracker.html.

—

15. Ryan Tarinelli, "Cuomo Softens COVID-19 Anti-Gathering Rule amid NYCLU Lawsuit," *New York Law Journal,* May 23, 2020.

16. *Wisconsin Legislature v. Palm,* 2020 Wis. 42 (2020).

17. Statement of Interest on Behalf of the United States, *Signature Sothbeys International Realty, Inc. v. Whitmer,* no. 1:20-cv-00360-PLM-PJG (W.D. Mich. 2020).

18. *South Bay United Pentecostal Church v. Gavin Newsom,* no. 20-55533, 2020 WL 2687079 (9th Cir. 2020), app. denied 2020 WL 2813056.

19. *Burwell v. Hobby Lobby Stores, Inc.*, 573 U.S. 682 (2014).

20. *Masterpiece Cakeshop, Ltd. v. Colorado Civil Rights Commission,* 138 S. Ct. 1719 (2018).

21. Ryan Martins, Shannon Price, and John Fabian Witt, "Contract's Revenge: The Waiver Society and the Death of Tort," 41 *Cardozo Law Review* 1265 (April 2020).

22. Frank M. Snowden, *Epidemics and Society: From the Black Death to the Present* 7 (2019).

23. Danielle Kaeble and Mary Cowhig, "Correctional Populations in the United States, 2016," *Bureau of Justice Statistics* (2018), https://www.bjs.gov/index.cfm?ty=pbdetail&iid=6226.

24. World Prison Brief, "United Kingdom: England and Wales," *Prison Studies* (2018), https://www.prisonstudies.org/country/united-kingdom-england-wales.

25. World Prison Brief, "China," *Prison Studies* (2016), https://www.prisonstudies.org/country/china.

26. Ashley Nellis, "The Color of Justice: Racial and Ethnic Disparity in State Prisons," in *The Sentencing Project,* June 14, 2016, https://www.sentencingproject.org/publications/color-of-justice-racial-and-ethnic-disparity-in-state-prisons/.

27. *Bell v. Wolfish,* 441 U.S. 520 (1979); *Rhodes v. Chapman,* 452 U.S. 337 (1981); Jacques Steinberg, "Doubling Up in Prison Cells Saves Money but Stirs Inmate Anger," *New York Times,* July 8, 1995, 21; Judith

Resnik, "Protecting Prisoners in Pandemics Is a Constitutional Must," *Bloomberg*, March 30, 2020.

28. William Barr, "Memorandum for Director of Bureau of Prisons," April 2, 2020.

29. Samantha Max, "Tennessee Department of Health Attributes Spike in Coronavirus Cases to Prison Outbreak," *WPLN News*, June 2, 2020; see also Samantha Max, "Tennessee Prison Criticized for Its COVID-19 Response," *National Public Radio*, June 2, 2020.

30. Jenny Hamel, "Inside Marion Correctional with COVID-19: 'We Just Passed It Around,'" *ideastream*, May 14, 2020, https://www.ideastream.org/news/inside-marion-correctional-with-covid-19-we-just-passed-it-around.

31. For example, *Laws of the Commonwealth of Pennsylvania, from the Fourteenth Day of October, One Thousand Seven Hundred* 5:274 (1812); *Revised Statutes of Mississippi* 1082 (1836).

32. Emily Widra and Peter Wagner, "While Jails Drastically Cut Populations, State Prisons Have Released Almost No One," Prison Policy Initiative, May 14, 2020, https://www.prisonpolicy.org/blog/2020/05/14/jails-vs-prison-update/; Kelan Lyons, "How COVID-19 Is Shrinking Connecticut's Prison Population," *CT Mirror*, May 1, 2020.

33. Dylan Segelbaum, "Wolf Announced a Temporary Reprieve Program: Fewer Than 150 Prisoners Have Been Released," *York Daily Record*, May 8, 2020.

34. Joseph Darius Jaafari and Vicky Taylor, "Inside a Pennsylvania Prison's Hunger Strike," *PA Post*, May 29, 2020.

35. Jamiles Lartey, "What COVID-19 Prison Outbreaks Could Teach Us about Herd Immunity," in *The Marshall Project*, June 1, 2020, https://www.themarshallproject.org/2020/06/01/what-covid-19-prison-outbreaks-could-teach-us-about-herd-immunity.

36. "Prison Official in Illinois Halts Malaria Research on Inmates," *New York Times*, April 28, 1974.

—

37. *United States v. Park,* no. 16-CR-473 (RA), 2020 WL 1970603 (S.D.N.Y. April 24, 2020); *United States v. Scparta,* no. 18-CR-578 (AJN), 2020 WL 1910481, at *1 (S.D.N.Y. April 20, 2020).

38. *Wilson v. Williams,* no. 4:20-cv-00794-JG (N.D. Oh. April 22, 2020).

39. *Livas v. Myers,* no. 2:20-CV-00422, 2020 WL 1939583 (W.D. La. April 22, 2020).

40. *In Re Petition of the Pennsylvania Prison Society, et al.,* no. 70-MM-2020 (M.D. Penn. April 3, 2020).

41. The COVID Tracking Project, "The COVID Racial Data Tracker," *Atlantic,* https://covidtracking.com/race (accessed June 5, 2020).

42. Graeme Wood, "What's Behind the COVID-19 Racial Disparity?" *Atlantic,* May 27, 2020; Cary P. Gross et al., "Racial and Ethnic Disparities in Population Level Covid-19 Mortality," *medRxiv,* May 11, 2020, https://www.medrxiv.org/content/10.1101/2020.05.07.2009 4250v1.full.pdf.

43. Maria Givens, "The Coronavirus Is Exacerbating Vulnerabilities Native Communities Already Face," *Vox,* March 25, 2020; Nicholas Kristof, "The Top U.S. Coronavirus Hot Spots Are All Indian Lands," *New York Times,* May 30, 2020; Joshua Cheetham, "Navajo Nation: The People Battling America's Worst Coronavirus Outbreak," *BBC News,* June 16, 2020.

44. Gregg Gonsalves and Amy Kapczynski, "The New Politics of Care," *Boston Review,* April 27, 2020.

45. Chandra L. Ford and Collins O. Airhihenbuwa, "Critical Race Theory, Race Equity, and Public Health," 100 *American Journal of Public Health* S30 (2010); Scott Burris, "Envisioning Health Disparities," 29 *American Journal of Law & Medicine* 151 (2003).

46. Abbe R. Gluck and Erica Turret, "Happy Tenth Birthday, Obamacare: This Crisis Would Be Much Worse without You," *Health Affairs Blog,* March 23, 2020; Abbe R. Gluck and Thomas Scott-Railton, "Affordable Care Act Entrenchment," 108 *Georgetown Law Journal* 495 (2020).

—

47. U.S. Bureau of Labor Statistics, "Labor Force Statistics from the Current Population Survey," https://www.bls.gov/web/empsit/cpsee _e16.htm (accessed June 7, 2020).

48. Elizabeth Arias, "Changes in Life Expectancy by Race and Hispanic Origin in the United States, 2013–2014," *NCHS Data Brief No. 244,* April 2016.

49. Raj Chetty et al., "The Association between Income and Life Expectancy in the United States, 2001–2014," 315 *JAMA* 1750 (2016).

50. Anti-Defamation League, "Reports of Anti-Asian Assaults, Harassment and Hate Crimes Rise as Coronavirus Spreads," *ADL Blog,* May 27, 2020, https://www.adl.org/blog/reports-of-anti-asian -assaults-harassment-and-hate-crimes-rise-as-coronavirus-spreads.

51. Michael Gentithes and Harold J. Krent, "Pandemic Surveillance – The New Predictive Policing," 12 *ConLawNOW* 57 (2020).

52. Max S. Kim, "South Korea Is Watching Quarantined Citizens with a Smartphone App," *MIT Technology Review,* March 6, 2020.

53. Olivier Nay, "Can a Virus Undermine Human Rights?" 5 *Lancet Public Health* 238 (2020).

54. Chris Yiu, "Technology and the Response to Covid-19: Our Approach," *Tony Blair Institute for Global Change,* April 3, 2020.

55. Zak Doffman, "Forget Apple and Google: Contact-Tracing Apps Just Dealt Serious New Blow," *Forbes,* May 12, 2020.

56. Doffman, "Forget Apple and Google."

57. Daniel Kahn Gillmor, "Principles for Technology-Assisted Contact-Tracing," April 16, 2020, https://www.aclu.org/sites/default/files /field_document/aclu_white_paper_-_contact_tracing_principles.pdf.

SUGGESTED READING

Ackerknecht, Edwin H. "Anticontagionism between 1821 and 1867." 22 *Bulletin of the History of Medicine* (1948).

Baldwin, Peter. *Contagion and the State in Europe, 1830–1930.* 2009.

Batlan, Felice. "Law in the Time of Cholera: Disease, State Power, and Quarantines Past and Future." 80 *Temple Law Review* (2007).

Benedict, Michael Les. "Contagion and the Constitution: Quarantine Agitation from 1859 to 1866." 12 *Journal of the History of Medicine* (April 1970).

Crosby, Alfred W. *America's Forgotten Pandemic.* 1989.

Downs, Jim. *Sick from Freedom: African-American Illness and Suffering during the Civil War and Reconstruction.* 2012.

Duffy, John. *The Sanitarians.* 1990.

Fenn, Elizabeth A. *Pox Americana: The Great Smallpox Epidemic of 1775–82.* 2001.

France, David. *How to Survive a Plague: The Inside Story of How Citizens and Science Tamed AIDS.* 2016.

—

SUGGESTED READING

Gonsalves, Gregg, and Amy Kapczynski. "The New Politics of Care." *Boston Review.* April 27, 2020.

Gostin, Lawrence O. *Public Health Law: Power, Duty, Restraint.* 2008.

Hartog, Hendrik. "Pigs and Positivism." 1985 *Wisconsin Law Review* (1985).

Hunter, Nan D. *The Law of Emergencies: Public Health and Disaster Management.* 2009.

Hunter, Tera. *To 'Joy My Freedom: Southern Black Women's Lives and Labors after the Civil War.* 1997.

Jones, Absalom, and Richard Allen. *A Narrative of the Proceedings of the Black People, during the Late Awful Calamity in Philadelphia, in the Year 1793: And a Refutation of Some Censures, Thrown upon Them in Some Late Publications.* 1794.

Mckiernan-González, John. *Fevered Measures: Public Health and Race at the Texas-Mexico Border, 1848–1942.* 2012.

Novak, William J. *The People's Welfare: Law and Regulation in Nineteenth-Century America.* 1996.

Olivarius, Kathryn. "Immunity, Capital, and Power in Antebellum New Orleans." 124 *American Historical Review* (2019).

Parmet, Wendy. *Populations, Public Health, and the Law.* 2009.

Roberts, Dorothy. *Fatal Invention: How Science, Politics, and Big Business Re-create Race in the Twenty-First Century.* 2012.

Roberts, Samuel Kelton. *Infectious Fear: Politics, Disease, and the Health Effects of Segregation.* 2009.

Rogers, Naomi. *Dirt and Disease: Polio Before FDR.* 1992.

Rosenberg, Charles E. *The Cholera Years: The United States in 1832, 1849, and 1866.* 1962.

Shah, Nayan. *Contagious Divides: Epidemics and Race in San Francisco's Chinatown.* 2001.

Snowden, Frank M. *Epidemics and Society: From the Black Death to the Present.* 2019.

—

SUGGESTED READING

Thornton, Russell. *American Indian Holocaust and Survival*. 1987.

Willrich, Michael. *Pox: An American History*. 2011.

ACKNOWLEDGMENTS

This book began as a lecture for my spring 2020 course American Legal History at Yale Law School. As COVID-19 shut down universities, and as courses went online to the virtual platform Zoom, I decided, at the urging of students, to add a session on the subject of the virus. Yale generously made the lecture public on its website. Adina Popescu Berk at Yale University Press saw the lecture and asked if I would expand it into a book. I hope she thinks it was worth it.

I was lucky to have the speedy help of brilliant law students as research assistants. Adela Lillolari, Paul Meosky, and Zoe Rubin were indefatigable in tracking down materials. Nat Warner helped me prepare the manuscript.

Early exchanges with Pedro Cantisano, Jim Downs, Abbe Gluck, Gregg Gonsalves, Bill Novak, Alan Olmstead, Steve Pitti, Judith Resnik, and Michael Willrich helped shape my thinking on the subject. Felice Batlan, Scott Burris, Amy Kapczynski, and Wendy Parmet generously read drafts. Feedback from the Yale Law School Faculty Workshop on Coronavirus and the Law provided valuable insight, as did the reactions

ACKNOWLEDGMENTS

of David Schorr and the participants in a Zoom conference, "The Legal History of Epidemics," hosted by the Buchmann Faculty of Law at Tel Aviv University. More generally, I leaned on the amazing historians who have produced a terrific secondary literature in the history of public health. Some of their names appear in the notes and occasionally in the text. Robin DuBlanc provided lightning-fast, superb copy edits. Errors of fact and deficiencies of judgment are mine.

Many thanks to Elliot Gerson, who offered encouragement at a critical moment; to the Witt Boys, Gus and Teddy, who sheltered in place and marched with me this spring; and to the astounding Beverly Gage, for being there.

—

INDEX

ACLU (American Civil Liberties
  Union), 61, 92, 137
ACT UP (AIDS Coalition to Unleash
  Power), 102
Affordable Care Act (2010), 112–13,
  119, 130
African Americans: COVID-19
  pandemic and, 108, 127–33;
  discriminatory nature of public
  health law for, 44–45; HIV/
  AIDS epidemic and, 47;
  immunization mandates and,
  77–78; incarceration rates for,
  47, 122; quarantinism and,
  55–56; Tuskegee syphilis study,
  45; unemployment rates for,
  131; yellow fever epidemic and,
  35–36, 38–39
AIDS. *See* HIV/AIDS
AIDS Coalition to Unleash Power
  (ACT UP), 102

Alabama: sanitationism in, 24; Tus-
  kegee syphilis study in, 45
Alien Labor Immigration Act (1891),
  51
American Civil Liberties Union
  (ACLU), 61, 92, 137
American Medical Association, 29
Americans with Disabilities Act
  (1990), 93
Angel Island (California), 49, 134
antibiotics, 88, 100
Anti-Mask League, 80, 82
Anti-Vaccination Society of America,
  75
Articles of Confederation, 16–17
Asian Americans, 133–34
Australia, COVID-19 pandemic in,
  136–37

Baldwin, Henry, 55
Baltimore: immunization mandates

in, 77–78; tuberculosis in, 44–45

Barnard, George, 65

Barr, William, 123

Bennett, William J., 90

Billings, John, 27–28, 33, 82

Bill of Rights, 5

bioterrorism, 106

Birdseye, Lucien, 67–68

Birx, Deborah, 110

Bliss, George, Jr., 63–67

border control. *See* immigration

Boston: anti-vaccination organizations in, 75; smallpox vaccinations in, 19

Bracero program, 52

Brandeis, Louis, 3–4

Brick Presbyterian Church v. Mayor of New York (1826), 24–25

bubonic plague, 6, 42

Buck v. Bell (1927), 59

Burroughs Wellcome, 101–2, 103

Burwell v. Hobby Lobby (2014), 118–19

California: anti-vaccination movement in, 76, 78; bubonic plague in, 42, 43–44; civil liberties in, 73; COVID-19 pandemic in, 110–11; flu epidemic (1918–19), 79–80; quarantinism in, 48, 49

cemetery regulations, 24–25, 118

Centers for Disease Control and Prevention (CDC), 90, 109

Chadwick, Edwin, 30–31

Chae Chan Ping v. United States (1889), 57

Chicago, public health powers in, 19

China: COVID-19 pandemic in, 108, 136; immigrants to U.S. from, 50–51, 57; incarceration rate in, 122

Chinese Exclusion Act (1882), 50–51, 57

cholera, 14, 39, 66

churches: cemetery regulations and, 24–25, 118; religious liberty and, 5, 117–19

Cicero, 19

civil liberties, 61–83; COVID-19 pandemic and, 61–63; infectious diseases and, 72, 81; mandatory immunizations and, 75–78; police power and, 67, 72, 82, 118; populist resentment of public health measures and, 75–80; poverty and, 93; public health policy and law vs., 63–74; sanitationism and, 85–106

compulsory sterilization, 59

Connecticut: COVID-19 pandemic in, 61, 125; smallpox in, 15–16

Constitution (U.S.), 5, 17

contact tracing, 135–37

COVID-19 pandemic, 107–37; decentralized power and, 108–13; incarcerated populations and, 121–27; judicial responses to, 113–21; racial inequities in, 127–33

INDEX

Cuba, yellow fever in, 53

Cuomo, Andrew, 61, 110, 114

decentralization of power, 111. *See also* state law and courts

detention for quarantines, 37, 41, 47–48. *See also* incarcerated populations

Deverell, William, 44

DeWine, Mike, 111

discrimination. *See* minorities; racial inequities

Douglass, Frederick, 77–78

Dowling, Joseph, 66

drug research, 98–104

DuBois v. Augusta (Ga. 1831), 54

Ebola, 85–86, 97

Eisenberg, Rebecca, 101

England: bubonic plague in, 6; incarceration rate in, 122

Equal Protection Clause, 74

face masks, 79–80, 121

Falwell, Jerry, 90

Fauci, Anthony, 110

Faulkner, William, 7

Field, Stephen, 57

Finlay, Carlos, 53

Fleming, Alexander, 88, 100

Florida, HIV/AIDS in, 90

Floyd, George, 139

flu epidemic (1918–19), 78–79

freedom of speech, 5

Georgia: civil liberties in, 69; quarantinism in, 54; sanitationism in, 21

Gibbons v. Ogden (1824), 22

Global Program on AIDS (WHO), 91

Gorgas, William, 53

Gostin, Lawrence, 91–93, 94; *Public Health Law,* 105

Grant, Ulysses S., 64

graveyard regulations, 24–25, 118

Griscom, John, 28

Harlan, John Marshall, 58–59, 60, 74, 82–83

Hartog, Hendrik, 21

Hassler, William, 79

health care system: access to, 130; drug research and, 98–104; health insurance and, 9, 113, 130

Heller, Michael, 101

Helms, Jesse, 46, 90, 96

Hickox, Kaci, 85–86, 97

Hirota, Hidetaka, 47

HIV/AIDS, 46–47, 88–106; pharmaceutical research on, 101–4

Holmes, Oliver Wendell, 59

hospitals, 23, 48, 55, 67–69, 116, 121

human rights, 91, 94

Hungary, COVID-19 pandemic in, 108

Hunt, Ward, 25

Hunter, Tera, 39

INDEX

hygiene, 26–27, 30, 82, 110, 140.
    See also sanitationism

Illinois: civil liberties in, 71; public
    health powers in, 19
immigration: COVID-19 pandemic
    and, 109–10, 121–27; quaran-
    tinism and, 47–53
immunizations: mandatory, 40,
    57–60, 73, 75–76; polio, 88,
    99; smallpox, 88, 99–100
incarcerated populations: COVID-
    19 pandemic and, 121–27;
    detention for quarantines, 37,
    41, 47–48; HIV/AIDS epidemic
    and, 47
Indiana: civil liberties in, 72–73;
    HIV/AIDS in, 90
infectious diseases: civil liberties
    and, 72, 81; drug research for,
    98–104; public policy and
    law influenced by, 1–2, 5–6;
    quarantinism and, 38, 45–46,
    49–51, 112; sanitationism and,
    15–17, 21–23, 26, 29, 97–98.
    See also specific diseases
intellectual property rights, 98–104
Isthmian Canal Commission (ICC),
    53

Jacobson, Henning, 58, 60, 76
Jacobson v. Massachusetts (1905),
    57–59, 74
jails. *See* incarcerated populations
Jenner, Edward, 75

Jew Ho v. Williamson (N.D. Cal.
    1900), 74
judicial responses to public health
    policy: on commerce power of
    Congress, 112–13; on COVID-
    19 pandemic, 113–21; on
    plenary power doctrine, 57–58;
    on police power, 3–4; on quar-
    antinism, 54–60; on religious
    liberty, 117–19. *See also* state
    law and courts; Supreme Court,
    U.S.; *specific cases*

Kansas, civil liberties in, 71
Kavanaugh, Brett, 119
Kelley, Florence, 29, 30
Koop, C. Everett, 46

Latinx: COVID-19 pandemic and,
    127, 129–30; HIV/AIDS
    epidemic and, 47; incarceration
    rates for, 47, 122
Leavitt, Judith Walzer, 42
life expectancy, 132
Locke, John: "Fundamental Constitu-
    tions," 15
Los Angeles, bubonic plague in,
    43–44
Louisiana: COVID-19 pandemic in,
    126; port quarantines in, 37;
    sanitationism in, 23–24; yellow
    fever in, 14, 39

Maine, civil liberties in, 69
Malcolm X, 78

INDEX

Mallon, Mary, 40–42

Mann, Jonathan, 90–91

March of Dimes, 99

Marine Hospital (New York), 48, 55, 67–68, 116, 121

Marion Correctional Institution (Ohio), 123

Marshall, George, 87

Marshall, John, 22, 27, 82

Marx, Karl, 2

Massachusetts: anti-vaccination organizations in, 75; immunization mandates in, 57–59, 75; quarantinism in, 47; sanitationism in, 19, 26–27, 31; smallpox vaccinations in, 19

Massachusetts Bay Colony, 36–37

Masterpiece Cakeshop v. Colorado Civil Rights Commission (2018), 119

Mckiernan-González, John, 52

McLean, John, 56

measles, 6

Meese, Edwin, 90

Metropolitan Board of Health (New York), 19, 25, 41, 64

Michigan: civil liberties in, 71, 72; COVID-19 pandemic in, 117, 121; sanitationism in, 18, 31

Minnesota: anti-vaccination organizations in, 76; civil liberties in, 71–72

minorities: anti-vaccination movement and, 77–78; COVID-19 pandemic and, 127–33; epidemic laws discriminating against, 42–47; incarceration rates for, 47, 122. *See also* racial inequities; *specific minority groups*

Mississippi, sanitationism in, 18

Morrow, William, 73–74

Murrow, Edward R., 99

Nathan, Alison, 126

National Cancer Institute, 101

National Consumers League, 29

National Council for Civil Liberties (UK), 92

National Federation of Independent Business v. Sebelius (2012), 112–13

National Foundation for Infantile Paralysis, 99

Native Americans: COVID-19 pandemic and, 127–28; smallpox and, 6; smallpox epidemic and, 38

Neuman, Gerald, 47

New Jersey, Ebola quarantines in, 85–86

New Orleans: port quarantines in, 37; sanitationism in, 23–24; yellow fever in, 14, 39

Newsom, Gavin, 110–11

New York: anti-vaccination movement in, 78; civil liberties in, 65–68, 71, 82; COVID-19 pandemic in, 61, 110, 114, 126; Ebola quarantines in, 85–86; Metropolitan Board of Health, 19, 25, 41, 64; *Passenger Cases* in, 55–56; port quarantines in, 37; quarantinism in, 47, 48; sanitationism in, 19–20, 24–25, 28, 29; typhus outbreak in, 40–41; yellow fever in, 14, 16

New York Civil Liberties Union, 114

New York Times on European immigrants after World War I, 51

Noem, Kristi, 128

North Carolina: civil liberties in, 68–69; sanitationism in, 21–22; smallpox in, 69

Novak, William, 24

Ohio, COVID-19 pandemic in, 111, 123, 126

Oklahoma, COVID-19 pandemic in, 121

Olivarius, Kathryn, 39

Orban, Viktor, 108

Oregon, anti-vaccination organizations in, 76

Pacific Mail Steamship Company, 49

Palm, Andrea, 114

Panama Canal, 53

Parmet, Wendy, 95–96, 103

partisanship, 107, 116–17, 121

Passenger Cases (1849), 55–56

patents on drugs, 99, 101–2

Patient Protection and Affordable Care Act (2010), 112–13, 119, 130

penicillin, 88, 100

Pennsylvania: anti-vaccination organizations in, 75; civil liberties in, 70; COVID-19 pandemic in, 125; port quarantines in, 37; sanitationism in, 21, 28; yellow fever in, 14, 17, 35, 39, 44

People v. See name of opposing party

pharmaceutical industry, 98–104

Philadelphia: anti-vaccination organizations in, 75; port quarantines in, 37; sanitationism in, 28; yellow fever in, 14, 17, 35, 44

plenary power doctrine, 3, 57–58

police power: civil liberties and, 67, 72, 82, 118; defined, 3–4; public health law and, 4–5, 112; sanitationism and, 22, 24

polio, 31–32, 88, 99

poverty: civil liberties and, 93; COVID-19 pandemic and, 128, 132; immunization mandates and, 40, 78; life expectancy and, 132; sanitationism and, 78, 93

prisons. *See* incarcerated populations

property rights, 5, 27, 98–104, 129–30

Public Health Service (U.S.), 45, 52–53, 88

quality-adjusted life years (QALYs), 132

quarantinism, 35–60; defined, 8; discrimination against minority populations, 42–47; HIV/AIDS and, 96; immigration and, 47–53; incarceration rates and, 122–23; judicial decisions on, 54–60; ports and, 36–38

racial inequities: in COVID-19 pandemic, 127–33; in public health policy and law, 42–47, 139–40; quarantinism and, 9, 10. *See also specific racial and ethnic groups*
Raimondo, Gina, 61–63
Reagan, Ronald, 46
Redfield, Robert, 109
religious liberty, 5, 117–19
Rhode Island, COVID-19 pandemic and, 61–63
Rhode Island Center for Freedom and Prosperity, 63
Roberts, John, 113
Robinson, Mary, 94
Roff, People v. (N.Y. 1856), 67–68
Rogers, Naomi, 32

Sabin, Albert, 99
Salk, Jonas, 88, 98–99
San Francisco: anti-vaccination movement in, 78; bubonic plague in, 42; civil liberties in, 73; flu epidemic (1918–19), 79–80; quarantinism in, 48, 49
sanitationism, 13–33; civil liberties and, 85–106; defined, 8; infectious diseases and, 15–17, 21–23, 26, 29, 97–98; police power and, 22, 24; poverty and, 78, 93; smallpox epidemic and, 13–16
SARS coronavirus outbreak (2003), 97–98

Schleicher, David, 108
September 11, 2001 terrorist attacks, 105
Shattuck, Lemuel, 31
Shaw, Lemuel, 22–23, 27
Sinclair, Upton, 30
Singapore, COVID-19 pandemic in, 136
Slaughter-House Cases (1866), 64
smallpox: civil liberties and, 69; immunization mandates for, 58–59, 71, 75–78, 88, 99–100; Native Americans and, 6; quarantines and, 38, 69; sanitationism and, 13–16
Snowden, Frank, 120–21
social distancing, 114
South Bay United Pentecostal Church v. Newsom (2020), 117–18, 119
South Korea, COVID-19 pandemic in, 135
state law and courts: police power and, 5, 105; quarantinism and, 47, 50, 54; sanitationism and, 16–18, 21, 23
stay-at-home orders, 110–11
Stern, Alexandra Minna, 52
Stewart, William H., 87
Sumner v. Philadelphia (E.D. Pa. 1873), 70
Supreme Court, U.S.: on commerce power of Congress, 112–13; COVID-19 pandemic case in, 117–18;

plenary congressional power doctrine and, 57–58; on police power, 3–4; on prison policy, 123; on quarantines, 54–60; on religious liberty, 117–19; on states' rights to regulate public health, 64, 107. *See also specific cases*

syphilis, 45

Taney, Roger, 56
Tebb, William, 75
Tennessee, COVID-19 pandemic in, 123
Tenth Amendment, 4
Texas: border health inspections in, 52, 139; COVID-19 pandemic in, 121
TraceTogether (app), 136
triaging systems, 132
Trump, Donald: Chinese graduate students banned by, 134
tuberculosis, 44–45
Turning Point Model State Public Health Act, 94–95
Tuskegee syphilis study, 45
"Typhoid Mary," 40–42
typhus, 40

unemployment, 131
United Kingdom: incarceration rate in, 122; National Council for Civil Liberties, 92. *See also* England
Utah, anti-vaccination organizations in, 76

vaccinations. *See* immunizations
ventilators, 131
Virginia, quarantinism in, 18
Visiting Nurse Service, 29

waivers for businesses reopening after shutdowns, 119–21
Wald, Lillian, 29, 30
Washington, George, 35
Whitmer, Gretchen, 117
WHO (World Health Organization), 88, 90–91
Willrich, Michael, 59
Wisconsin: anti-vaccination organizations in, 76; civil liberties in, 71; COVID-19 pandemic in, 114–17
Wong Wai v. Williamson (N.D. Cal. 1900), 73–74
World Health Organization (WHO), 88, 90–91
Wright, Lawrence: *The End of October,* 123–24

Xi Jinping, 108

yellow fever, 14, 17, 35, 52

Zaire, HIV/AIDS epidemic in, 90–91